Praise for

Driving Down Cost

"Fills an amazingly large gap in the business book universe, with substance and insight. Read it to stay ahead, in tough times and good times."
Chris Outram, Founder & Partner, OC&C Strategy Consultants

"Driving down cost has long been the neglected Cinderella of management, but Wileman's book makes it the Belle of the Ball. Brilliant!"
Richard Koch, entrepreneur-investor and author of the bestselling The 80/20 Principle

"Wileman is the man with the fearless scissors. But, like the Pink Floyd advice, he is also 'careful with that axe, Eugene'."
Matthew Gwyther, Editor of Management Today

"An incisive and engrossing read on what could be a dry business topic. Understanding cost is at the heart of good management."
Geoff Cooper, CEO of Travis Perkins

"Topical, practical and very entertaining. Well worth its own cost."
Charles Wilson, CEO of Booker Group

To my family – Jill, Alex, Charlie and Billie – who have taught me the love of cost control.

Driving Down Cost

How to Manage and Cut Costs
– Intelligently

ANDREW WILEMAN

nb

NICHOLAS BREALEY
PUBLISHING

LONDON · BOSTON

First published by
Nicholas Brealey Publishing in 2008

3–5 Spafield Street
Clerkenwell, London
EC1R 4QB, UK
Tel: +44 (0)20 7239 0360
Fax: +44 (0)20 7239 0370

20 Park Plaza, Suite 1115A
Boston
MA 02116, USA
Tel: (888) BREALEY
Fax: (617) 523 3708

www.nicholasbrealey.com
www.drivingdowncost.net

ISBN 978-1-85788-512-5

British Library Cataloguing in Publication Data
A catalogue record for this book is available from the
British Library.

FSC

Printed in Finland by WS Bookwell
on Forest Stewardship Council certified paper.

Contents

CONTENTS

1

Preface

This book sets out a structured, practical approach to intelligent cost management. It contains:

○ A cost manager's toolkit of key ideas and cost-management strategies.
○ Frameworks for analyzing cost.
○ Practical techniques for implementing cost-reduction programs – one-off or continuous.

The book addresses the topic of cost in a general and holistic way. It is relevant to all private-sector businesses and to public-sector organizations. However, there is a bias in the material toward service businesses and service activities rather than manufacturing. This is because there is a great deal new to say about service cost whereas production cost already has a rich literature.

Driving Down Cost is for the general manager and the general reader, providing an overview of the broad sweep of cost management rather than detailed coverage of specialist subtopics. So for example I discuss procurement, but not at the level of detail needed to become a professional procurement manager. I discuss management accounts, but not with the degree of finesse expected of a CPA or finance director. There are dozens of detailed technical manuals available on procurement and on cost and management accounting and that is not what this book is about.

One of my motivations for writing was that I could not think of any book that sets out a generalized approach to the topic of cost management. I checked out my top-of-the-head view on Amazon and Google and found that it was right. Given that so many consulting projects, and so much management energy and attention, are focused on cost reduction, this gap was surprising. It gave me reason to believe that this book would find a good audience.

Managing Cost or Cutting Cost?

I and my publishers had a chewy debate on whether the book should talk about *cutting* cost or *managing* cost.

"Managing" was gray and dull. A book on "cost management" could sound like a cure for insomnia, passive and stodgy, sterile accounting.

"Cutting" seemed a lot sexier: dashing swordplay, testosterone leadership, thrusting interventions, the Errol Flynn of business topics.

However, you only need to engage in high-profile cost *cutting* if you haven't been effective at long-haul cost *management*. Cost cutting sounds like something you have to do in extremis, as part of a one-off cost-reduction program. This book does cover such one-off programs but they're not its main theme. Most managers are very interested in sustained cost management and less interested in one-off cost cutting.

Therefore managing is the main theme and cutting the secondary theme of the book.

This still left us unfortunately with an insomnia challenge around the title, which we have cunningly sidestepped with *Driving Down Cost*, making this the *Top Gear* of cost-management books.

The Research Base

I call on several sources for the book's analysis and conclusions.

First, I draw on my own experience as a consultant and line manager. I started as a business consultant in the mid-1970s, working with Booz Allen Hamilton in London and New York and with Boston Consulting Group in Boston while I got my Harvard MBA. I ended up as a senior partner with OC&C Strategy Consultants in Europe.

I have run at least 50 big one-time cost-reduction projects, mainly in America and Europe plus a few in Asia. My client has always been the CEO, another board-level manager or the head of a business unit. Recently my clients have included new private equity owners. These projects and clients have covered many business sectors: consumer goods, retailing, travel and transport, financial services, software and IT, information and media services, telecommunications, commercial services.

With those cost-reduction projects the client usually needs to get cost out quickly but without killing future growth potential. A project will take three to four months. We set up working parties with management teams, do the analysis, identify cuts, develop action programs. It is an iterative and argumentative process. I have done it for big global businesses with billion-dollar cost bases and thousands of staff, and for small individual departments with 50 staff.

I have also been CFO of two technology businesses, a software firm based in Seattle and an offshore IT business in India. And I have been strategy director and manager of strategic projects for a global travel business, for one of the UK's top physical distribution and retail businesses and for a fashion and department store retailer. In these positions I have managed cost over the long haul, under regular planning, budgeting and reporting cycles.

Material was also developed specifically for this book. There are several case studies, both company stories and projects, and there are interviews with senior business figures reflecting on good and not-so-good approaches to cost management. Last, there have been working sessions with my *alma mater* consulting firm OC&C Strategy Consultants, with which I still work as an adviser and which has contributed critiques of my frameworks and points of view.

Who the Book Is For

The book is for managers at every level and in every function.

Cost management is not an issue only for the CEO or for senior management. Junior managers who are proactively tight on cost are learning good habits for the future, ones that will bring them recognition and advance their climb up the organizational chart.

Senior managers promote people who make tough decisions themselves and take full responsibility for those decisions. They advance people who come up with solutions, not problems. Too many junior managers take a long time to get to that coming-of-age realization. They prefer cosy after-work drinks with their teams, telling their staff that it's the boss making nasty decisions about not funding extra resources or getting rid of underperformers. They will still be having those cozy drinks in 10 years' time, when their take-it-on-the-chin cost-cutter colleague is in the boardroom.

And cost management is not an issue only for the functions of finance, production control or customer call centers. The HR department, formerly full of personnel careerists who "just love working with people", is now staffed with hard-nosed cost managers whose task is to help manage that most difficult category, people cost. Marketing departments no longer think that all problems could be solved by doubling the ad spend, they think about how to get much higher returns from fewer marketing dollars. Even investment bankers and sales reps are getting cost conscious about expenses... actually delete that, I got carried away there for a moment.

Most of the case studies in the book are about quite large businesses, of the size of a Fortune 500 or FTSE 250 company. But the ideas and actions are equally valid for smaller organizations. Indeed, for small private companies and their owner-operators the cost imperative is very direct and personal.

While most of the material is about private-sector businesses I conclude with a chapter on the public sector, where cost management can be a huge challenge. So I hope that the book also finds an audience, and a usefulness, among public-sector managers and policy makers.

How the Book Is Structured

- ○ **Chapter 1 – Good Cost Management** looks at the unsung hero the cost manager, and at how intelligent cost management helps an organization's operations be both cheaper *and* better.
- ○ **Chapter 2 – Cost Leadership** considers how the top team – the CEO, chief operating officer, business unit heads, the heads of finance and HR – needs to take the lead and set the tone on cost.
- ○ **Chapter 3 – Techniques and Tactics** lays out a set of ideas, approaches, tips and tricks that I have found effective in cost-reduction programs and in ongoing cost management.
- ○ **Chapter 4 – People** tackles the most difficult and most critical cost area: full-time staff. Because it is problematic, it is usually left until last in any cost discussion. I take it on early.
- ○ **Chapter 5 – Suppliers** covers all the other cost categories, from raw materials to outsourced services.
- ○ **Chapter 6 – Cost Cutting Case Study** gives a blow-by-blow account of a four-month cost-reduction project I managed for a European business services company that had been acquired by private equity.

○ **Chapter 7 – Wired and Global** explores two of today's high-profile cost-reduction themes that have huge potential: the internet and globalization (the China model and the India model). In a decade or two they may be played out, but right now they are incredibly powerful.

○ **Chapter 8 – Lateral Thinking** turns some conventional thinking about cost on its head. It looks at the sneaky ways cost can be created and the smart ways it can be cut – like getting your customers to do your work for you or turning cost into revenue.

○ **Chapter 9 – Cost Management as Strategy** discusses how good cost management can underpin business strategy, including delivering value via acquisitions, using pricing as a competitive weapon and discovering more new growth opportunities.

○ **Chapter 10 – Cost in the Public Sector** employs the analytical framework of the previous chapters to look at the particular challenges of managing and cutting cost in government spending.

○ **Conclusion** summarizes how the various parts of the cost manager's toolkit fit together.

Business Book Cycles

Sometimes cost management is in fashion, sometimes it's out.

I love *The Economist*. As I grow older I suspect I no longer have any opinions of my own, just what I read in its pages. But even the excellent *Economist* is caught by the vagaries of business fashion. In May 2002, as businesses hunkered down after the Nasdaq crash and 9/11, it ran a big feature arguing that "Cost-cutting is not just for downturns, but for always". Then three years later the worm turned. An editorial in April 2005 argued that "Companies should shift their attention from cost-cutting to business-building".

So is this the wrong business book at the wrong point in the cycle? Should I be writing (and you be buying) a book on growth, innovation and team building?

No. *The Economist* had it right the first time: Cost management is not just for downturns but for always. Cost strategies and growth strategies need each other; they are joined at the hip.

And as it happens, as I'm finishing this final draft in early 2008 the US, the UK and other big western economies are looking decidedly shaky, sick from the credit binge. So a cost-cutting wave really looks imminent and this book is highly topical.

No need to hesitate. Buy now!

The Cost Manager's Toolkit

PDA-size Summary

LEADERSHIP	Challenging base case
	Individual accountability
	Persistence
	A continuous improvement culture
	Short timeframes
	Feedback loops
	Strategic skepticism
	Top team – Finance, HR
	Role models
TECHNIQUES AND TACTICS	Understanding cost dynamics
	Management accounts and metrics
	Bang for buck
	Slice and dice
	Understanding natural cost trends
	Cash cost vs P&L cost
	Best practice
	Competitive analysis
PEOPLE	Hiring
	Paying
	Technology and productivity
	Firing
	Minimizing the core
SUPPLIERS	Playing the balance of power
	Fewer better suppliers
	Intelligent negotiation
	Avoiding lock-in
	Managing total cost of ownership
	Tough on services cost
	Reduce non-labor overhead
WIRED AND GLOBAL	The internet – costs of interaction
	Globalization – the China card
	Globalization – the India card
LATERAL THINKING	Time is money
	Complexity is expensive
	Quality cuts cost
	Let customers do the work
	Turn cost into revenue
COST MANAGEMENT AS STRATEGY	Deliver value on acquisitions
	Underpin pricing strategies
	Discover more new growth opportunities
	Create an effective center in a large corporation

1

Good Cost Management

Capitals are increased by parsimony, and diminished by prodigality and misconduct.
—Adam Smith, *The Wealth of Nations*, 1776

There is intelligent cost management and there is bad cost management. For instance, it would be immoral to cut costs in a way that increases risk for customers, for staff or for society at large. Low-cost airlines cannot scrimp on aircraft maintenance. Chemical producers must make factories safe and dispose of hazardous waste. Rail networks need to maintain their tracks. Bad cost cutting in these areas would be unethical and actually uneconomic: the potential cost of any disaster would overwhelm the short-term savings.

It would be near-sighted and stupid not to put a high value on relationships and trust – between a business and its customers, and between a business and its staff. Clothing retailers could reduce cost by being hard-nosed on accepting product returns, but they would lose customer loyalty and future business. Companies could treat their workers as hire-and-fire commodities, but they would decrease quality, productivity and community goodwill. These kinds of calculations are right both morally and economically. Caring for customers and nurturing employees are not at odds with good cost management.

The harder calculations are around distinguishing good investment in future growth from bad excessive cost today. Being able to do this effectively is one of the core skills of an intelligent cost cutter. It is easy in almost any business to take a quick hack at costs like marketing, new business development teams, loss-making early-stage investments, store renovation programs – costs with an uncertain future payback. But although good cost management is a necessary characteristic of a great company, it is not sufficient. Great companies need profitability now *and* platforms for future growth, and that is what this book is all about.

The Unsung Hero

I have a deep respect for good cost management. Building a lean muscular business, stripping out fat… this is hard but very rewarding. I like seeing staff get more productive, being able to do more with their time, becoming more effective. And I like getting tough with suppliers, in a tough-but-fair kind of way.

The bit I don't like, which nobody likes, is getting rid of people, downsizing, streamlining. But that is probably the essence of good cost management. And it earns my deepest respect, because it is difficult and emotional and most people duck it.

A good cost manager is an unsung hero. Management books and magazines are full of articles on strategy, growth, culture, organization, financial engineering. You can read *Fortune* or *Forbes* or *The Economist* for a year and not come across an article that's mainly about cost management. You can look down Amazon's list of best-selling business books and they're all about leadership, core competencies, governance, innovators' dilemmas – nothing about cutting costs.

I'm looking at a book called *A Manager's Guide to Leadership*, which is a text for executive training programs at Ashridge Management College near London. The book lists 14 "key leadership challenges". 13 are about lovely things like innovation, learning organizations, teams, social responsibility. Tucked away at number 9 is the only cost-related challenge, coyly entitled "streamlining".

In fact, most managers I know spend half their time and brain-power on costs: how to stop them growing like Topsy, where and how much to cut, how to get the management team focused on driving them down, whether any cuts are too deep. So there is a gap between what business books think is in managers' brains and what is really in them.

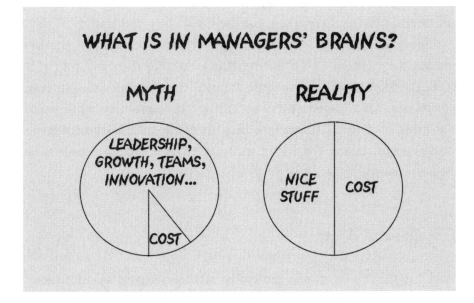

WHAT IS IN MANAGERS' BRAINS?

MYTH

REALITY

LEADERSHIP, GROWTH, TEAMS, INNOVATION...

COST

NICE STUFF

COST

Dilbert's pointy-haired boss takes this to the other extreme. In one strip he is deep in thought: "Hmm. If I cut costs enough, I can make money on no revenue."

Business success is about both growth *and* cost. Growth is exciting for everybody: managers, staff, stock analysts, journalists. Cost is dull and depressing. But the reality is like golf: drive for show, putt for dough. Growth is the fat driver, the Big Bertha, smack the ball down the fairway 300 yards and you're a Tiger. Cost management is the putter, the six-footers that keep not quite dropping in, then you're five strokes off the leader and it's too late to come back.

Private equity is a good example. Private equity investors take unloved bits of public quoted firms, or even whole firms in the doldrums, and squeeze gold out of them. How do they perform this alchemy? They do some strategic repositioning, divesting unpromising or distracting business lines, reinvesting in fewer areas of high potential. They take on more debt. They put in stronger incentives for a few top managers. But their main sorcerer's stone is straightforward cost reduction. They strip out a tonne of cost. They ruthlessly and relentlessly attack every cost line, particularly head office and overhead costs (except their own fees, naturally).

If you take a low-growth business with a 5% operating profit margin and take out 10% of the costs, you've tripled the margin to 15% (OK, 14.5% actually, before the finance team jumps in – strategy consultants are allowed a bit of rounding). If you do that while keeping most of your customers, selling off some secondary businesses or assets and taking on a load more debt, you can quintuple your equity investment in a few years.

Cheaper and Better

Back in the 1970s it was generally accepted that a good strategy involved clear choices. You couldn't be all things to all people. You couldn't keep all your options open.

In particular, you couldn't be cheaper *and* better. As Michael Porter put it back then, you had to choose between a low cost strategy and a differentiation strategy. Differentiation generally meant being better (or being perceived as better) and more expensive. This polarized choice was seen as capturing how customers behave and how firms have to compete. It was even seen as true of countries. You could choose high-quality and very expensive machine tools from Germany or cheap and not very reliable tools from (this was the 1970s) Japan.

Then the Japanese changed the whole game. They moved up from low cost entry points and became the benchmark for quality, reliability, top-end design, branding – everything associated with differentiation. Honda and Toyota set new quality standards in cars, trouncing GM and Ford. The same story played out in televisions and audio, in cameras, in bicycle gears. The Japanese showed that the killer play was to be cheaper *and* better.

More recently, New World wines have knocked the French off the top of the heap on quality and cost. Dell's 1990s leadership in PCs was based on high efficiency and low cost combined with superior customer service.

There are exceptions where customers still need to see high cost as a signal of quality, like perfume, cosmetics, high-end fashion goods; or like investment banking, consulting, legal services. But most businesses now strive to be cheaper *and* better; customers look for products and solutions that are cheaper *and* better. Tight cost management is seen not as opposed to high quality but as part and parcel of it.

The same polarization used to be discussed around company cultures. You could either be a caring, nurturing company or you could be a hard-ass cost cutter. Who would want to work for the latter? How could you expect to attract and retain talent?

Nevertheless, this is another false choice. It turns out that talented employees generally prefer demanding employers. They want to work in well-managed, profitable businesses. They don't want underperformers cuddled and cosseted.

Managing and Cutting Costs – Intelligently

This is why good cost management is so critical. It takes a great deal of time and energy to build sales and loyal customers. It's hard to rely on revenue from one quarter to another. But costs, on the other

LANGUAGE MATTERS

I used an example from Ashridge earlier to illustrate the weighting of nice vs nasty topics on leadership courses. It also illustrates how some cost-related terms have come to be accepted as good and virtuous while others conjure up the Dark Side:

○ **Good and virtuous**: eliminating waste, increasing productivity, public-sector "reform" (a peculiar UK euphemism for cutting over-staffed public-sector jobs), streamlining.
○ **Dark Side**: Cost cutting, downsizing, asset stripping, redundancy, termination.

Everybody loves the idea of productivity gains, focusing on "more from the same", not lingering on the equally likely idea of "the same from less". And everybody disapproves of waste, with its strong enviro-eco connotations and its Darwinian backbone.

hand: you don't need to be a rocket scientist to get that side of the business under control. What is most frustrating is when the revenue is coming through but you're blowing the cost line. There shouldn't be any excuse for that.

Through the whole dot-com boom and bust around the year 2000 it was as if an entire generation of managers, investors and commentators had never heard of cost management. They were on a New Paradigm high when what they needed was a Cost 101 refresher course.

Waste is very annoying. Think of executives on change management programs at $10,000 a pop; governments squandering billions on bad IT projects; Christmas presents dumped in the trash.

And cost management really is strategic. It's not a question of choosing between growth and cost cutting. Being a good cost manager gives you the platform to be strategic. It buys you time to make mistakes and build revenue, margin to outprice your competitors, funds to outinvest them.

I used to be a full-time strategy consultant. Like any good strategy consultant I liked thinking about Big Strategy Questions. On one study I did at BCG in its intellectual heyday, we spent some months considering whether containers were defined by what they kept *in* or what they kept *out*. So I got on my high horse when later, at OC&C Strategy Consultants, my commendably sales-oriented partner Chris harpooned some juicy projects to cut office overhead. "That's not strategy," I huffed. "We can't do that kind of grunt work – the cost of paper clips indeed!"

How wrong I was. It is immensely satisfying to cut the cost of paper clips by 20%. It can actually be more satisfying than exploring the Platonic essence of Tetrapak. In this book I explain how and why.

2

Cost Leadership

I call that bold talk for a one-eyed fat man.

—Robert Duvall to John Wayne, *True Grit*

Strong leadership is a prerequisite for good cost management. Cost leadership starts with the CEO or business unit head and cascades down through the top management team. They need to build a tough cost culture and be good role models in their personal behavior. They need two key staff functions to be very active supporters of cost control – finance and HR.

Imprinting a tough attitude to cost right down through the organization takes True Grit. It takes a Rooster Cogburn CEO.

A Challenging Base Case

Your base case position, what you expect in terms of cost trend, will be a big contributor to the cost outcome.

For example, you could start off the annual budget process by telling your business unit heads that this is a year of prudent consolidation, that they should plan on no headcount additions but a 3–4% increase in cost per head plus some small reductions in bought-in costs, and that with that cost base they should be able to manage some modest revenue growth.

Or you could say, revenue growth is looking difficult this year so I want to see 5% productivity gains, which means that we plan on headcount coming down by 5%, but I don't want to see any reduction in the revenue plan.

Those are two very different base case positions. Under the first scenario, management gets the message that they can relax a little, they can tread water, put off nasty decisions, do some strategic thinking. Under the second, their feet are being held to the fire. There's no standing still. If they're not growing revenue they'd better be cutting costs – either way, the base case position is that you expect 5% (or whatever percentage works) productivity growth, every year. If you don't stay paranoid, keep moving forward, your competitors will overtake you.

Once this kind of base case behavior is established, managers will stop coming to budget reviews with a business-as-usual, status quo budget. They will know that won't survive one minute in the CEO review. The whole tone of the business will have changed.

When you're doing a house renovation your builders find out fast if you're a soft touch. At the end of Week 1 they put in for an extra $10,000 because you've altered the handles on the cupboards and obviously that's changed the whole project. Roll over on that and you are looking at a $50,000 overspend by the end of the month. But if your base case is no, you guys accommodate that in the original budget, you can stop cost escalation.

As a strong cost leader, your base case expectation must be for real productivity gains and other unit cost reductions every year. Repeat that message and stick by it, until it is taken as a given by your management team and pushed down by them to the rest of the organization.

Individual Accountability

To drive down cost you need clear accountability and good reporting. When your management team is sitting round the table, you need to be able to attach specific cost targets to individual names in such a way that those individuals really control the outcome. And then there must be the possibility of tracking results in the same way.

Individual accountability is not the same as shared or group accountability. Individual accountability is much better.

Say you are CEO of a traditional phone company, with a mix of declining fixed-line and growing mobile business. Overall, revenue and profits are heading down. Cost needs cutting and you've got a good list of ideas.

But your top management structure is a matrix of heads of customer segments (like home, small business, large corporate) and heads of line functions (like customer service, network operations, marketing). Organizing around customer segments was a hot idea a few years ago. It seemed to work well in a brighter, growing market, when the matrix complexities were managed in a good team spirit.

However, in a tougher cost-control environment the matrix team approach doesn't work. Every cost initiative you come up with ends up having three or four names tagged to it as "responsible". When you review progress at the next management meeting, it's not clear who should be reporting on it or who gets shouted at for lack of progress. It's not even very obvious what data you are tracking to follow progress. When the progress isn't there everybody looks at everybody else. None of the three or four managers really feels responsible.

For tough cost management you have to have single primary accountability. One person takes on the targets and reports on the results. Those targets and results are treated as being primarily under that person's control.

If you need to break up old management accounts formats to achieve this, then do so. For example, in the past the head of engineering may have reported on the full cost of engineering including facilities. But under an aggressive cost-reduction program the reality is that Finance controls facility decisions and outcomes. So while you are in tough cost management mode, Finance reports on facilities cost and Engineering reports only on headcount and headcount-related cost. The conversations are clear, short and effective.

There are so many problems when this approach is not taken. Companies organized for growth and innovation have to move into a colder era of cost management. The collegiate approach that served them well in the past becomes a liability.

Cost control is a pretty thankless and unattractive activity and people will dodge tough decisions if they can. Team accountability only makes ducking and delaying easier.

Persistence

It's a long road baby, but I'm gonna find the end.
Picked up my bag baby, and I tried it again.

—Bessie Smith

When CEOs and managers ask "Is there a secret to getting cost out?" they are thinking of sexy concepts like activity-based costing, zero-based budgeting, reengineering, life-cycle costing. These can be useful but they are not the key to success. The key to success is annoyingly simple: persistence.

You ask the same question again and again. You push for better results and you keep on pushing. This is true for a manager, a consultant working around management on a cost-reduction project, or a non-executive board member challenging the CEO.

A friend of mine is a partner in private equity in London. Cost cutting is a key part of how private equity firms extract more value from businesses. My friend says the only key ingredient for success in cost cutting is persistence. Once managers understand that the cost questions are going to get asked again and again, that they will be pushed and pushed until they achieve serious results, they find new cost-reduction ideas to put on the table.

I was working with an American company in Miami on a project to cut the cost base by 15%. (The target is almost always 15% – it sounds nasty but achievable.) I was working through the management group on my initial rounds of interviews and as usual everyone was stonewalling. They were offering painless 2 or 3% savings, like flying coach rather than business or canceling the customer conference that year – also normal tactics.

The first one to crack was the customer service manager. We were on about our third-round interview and she said, "You know, I've been thinking about this, and if I'm really honest and smart about it I reckon I can get more than 15%, I can get 20% of the cost out, with some pain and some risk. Here's how I could do it..."

I remember that process very clearly, because all I'd really done in that series of interviews was turn up smiling and keep on saying, "We just have to find ways to get these cost savings, we just have to find ways to get these cost savings." And she rose to the challenge.

Other managers stonewalled for longer or never came up with the goods. The customer service manager powered up in the outside lane and was CEO five years later. She was obviously CEO material from her performance in those early interviews, and she has carried on being as persistent with her management team.

Once the people in your organization believe that you'll keep on asking until you get a good answer, they'll come up with the goods. But you have to earn that belief with tenacity and single-mindedness.

The opposite is also true. If people know that you can be snowed or deflected, if they know that you'll forget to follow up meeting after meeting or that every review will bring a new CEO *idée du jour*, then you're dead in the water on cost management.

The next three themes are really all subsets of this overarching theme of persistence and drive: a CI culture, short timeframes and feedback loops.

A Continuous Improvement Culture

Continuous improvement, or CI in shorthand, is a management approach that gained currency in the 1980s and 1990s. Some of it came from Japanese production methods focusing on quality and production cost. It included the notion of embedding a CI mentality right down to the most junior job levels, so the janitor became as involved as the plant manager.

With a CI culture nobody in the organization ever thinks OK, now we've achieved this year's cost targets let's just run things steadily for a bit, no more changes. A CI culture implies there's always a next idea or a next step, however small. And it says that if you're not moving a little bit further forward in some way, there's a danger you'll start slipping back – if not in absolute terms then relative to your competitors. You have to be paranoid about complacency.

And with a CI culture, nobody ever thinks OK, there's more to do, but I'll wait for a few months and assemble a good long, meaty to-do list, then I'll really go for it, I'll make a sprint for the tape. A CI culture says do even a little bit today, don't wait for a major event, a big process – if you do, there's a risk it won't happen, it could become too monumental and hard to handle. (This is actually a pretty good approach for your personal life too.)

I work with a distribution business in the UK that really has embedded a strong CI culture. The senior management team can sleep a lot better at night if they know that right down through the

THE GOD OF SMALL PERCENTAGES

Underlying the CI idea is an understanding of the power of compounding even small improvements year on year.

Say you can get your unit costs to decline by 1% a year. Getting that improvement takes a lot of effort. You might feel frustrated and that it's not a big enough prize for all the effort.

But say your competitor, who isn't making quite the same effort, can only hold its unit costs flat. Within five years you will have built up a 5% cost advantage. If you pass half of that on to customers you'll take share from the competitor – and your increasing relative scale will accelerate your cost advantage momentum. Project that trend out ten years and your competitor is dead.

Strategic cost managers worship the God of compounded small percentages.

layers of organization people are owning this as their challenge and are doing something about it every day.

Short Timeframes

This is part of a CI culture but it's important enough to highlight. Good cost reduction never got achieved with a five-year plan. Cost reduction gets achieved when you push for fast results.

Over the last 30 years one of the big changes in business has been the compression of planning timeframes. This is true for exotic activities like strategic planning. One of my earliest consulting assignments in the late 1970s was a strategic planning review for a big UK corporate where we developed 10-year and 20-year financial scenarios! In most of my work now with technology companies we focus on the next quarter's financial targets in detail, and our strategic planning horizon is the following 12 months.

The same timeframe compression has occurred in cost management. Thirty years ago I might have seen a plan where some core costs drifted down gradually over three to five years, or where an overstaffing situation was slowly unwound over several years by quiet natural attrition. These days the question would be what progress we can make on those costs in the next week, the next month, enough if we have to bite some painful bullets.

Feedback Loops

A good cost manager needs good feedback loops. You have to know where you're making progress, where the shortfalls are, whether you're on target and on time. This is a variation on the old saw "what gets measured gets managed". We could add to that "what gets measured quickly, and gets reviewed quickly, gets managed well and fast".

A good feedback loop requires good data. You need to be able to see the hard, concrete facts around progress or the lack of it versus key targets. The numbers have to be reliable and easy to interpret, so that managers don't waste time debating what they mean but focus instead on what more needs to be done.

A good feedback loop must be timely. Outcomes have to be known quickly and reported on regularly.

And a good feedback loop involves visibility and transparency. The numbers, good or bad, should be out on the table for all managers to see and discussion should be in open forum.

FEEDBACK LOOPS: A BRIDGE TOO FAR
You can take the feedback loop thing too far. I was once working on a cost-reduction program for a private equity business across

Europe. The private equity partner set up a bi-weekly reporting process that was intended to ratchet up the pressure for concrete results, very fast, with targets signed off and delivered by all the local country managers. The only problem was, the cycle left us no time actually to do any of the cost-reduction work. He demanded that every target, and every report of progress versus target, be signed off in advance of the meeting by all the managers involved, and that the numbers were all reconciled – in advance – with a pan-European rolling budget being maintained by the central finance team.

It was an absolute nightmare. We'd have a meeting on Monday of Week 1. Then we'd spend two days agreeing what we'd agreed in the meeting and send out a write-up by Thursday morning of Week 1. By the following Thursday (Week 2) we had to send out papers in advance of our next bi-weekly review the following Monday (Week 3). Those papers had to be signed off and reconciled with everybody in the lower ranks, so we had to do that by about Tuesday of Week 2. That left us only around two working days (basically the middle weekend) in which to find any cost-saving ideas and figure out how to implement them. Surreal.

Strategic Skepticism

One word is guaranteed to make the true cost manager's ears prick up and their skin crawl: strategic.

You're at the table for the monthly management meeting and there it is. The sales director has just said that sales target XYZ is a strategic customer. Uh-oh.

The sales director says that XYZ offers huge long-run potential. Future sales will be massive and highly profitable because they'll be locked in. *And* it's a reference account that will open up whole new market segments. *And* there's no way you can let the competition get a look in. "But of course, on this deal, right now, our first big sale with them, obviously we have to give it away. I'm offering a very aggressive price, and I'm throwing in a three-year support package free."

When sales guys start talking about strategic customers, you should suspect that:

○ They've been wining and dining the account for months and now they need to make a commission.
○ Or the sales director needs this sale to hit budget for the quarter.
○ The customer won't buy at any price that makes you any money.
○ If you open the account relationship at this price level, next year they'll want a deeper price cut.
○ And they'll tell all their competitors, so those potential accounts will want the same zero-profit deal when you try selling to them.
○ The best thing you can do to hurt your competitors is to let them win this account.

This is a good starting position, true in 90% of cases. In the other 10% there might really be a reason to lose money on a deal to create future opportunities. That's OK, let those exceptions prove their case.

If it's not a strategic customer, it might be a strategic investment. Another righteous shudder ripples through the cost cutter. The head of strategy just stood up to make a pitch for a strategic investment. Ignore all the guff about market positioning and future options value. Here's the real subtext:

○ I've tried, but even with massive manipulation of the numbers I can't justify the following investment proposal on any reasonable analysis of the economics and the financials.
○ But this is really a sexy technology/it's a great story for the analysts/we've had some great dinners with the founders/I'm a bit bored with our core business.
○ So I'd like to do it anyway and do you have confidence in me or not?

Another favorite back in the heady dot-com bubble days, and not unknown today, is a strategic partnership. This is usually sponsored by the head of business development. Biz Dev, as it became known, floats in a vague netherworld somewhere between sales, marketing and strategy. People there sort of have commercial roles but aren't actually accountable for anything. So they spend a lot of time on strategic partnerships.

In the high-tech world strategic partnerships are things you announce on your website that sound sexy, but after one minute of reflection are obviously meaningless or impractical. They can be between major direct competitors – as in Accenture announces a strategic partnership with IBM or SAP with Oracle. Or they may be with your supplier of office stationery. Or some bloke you met on a plane to Australia who said he wouldn't mind becoming a distributor.

The one common characteristic of strategic partnerships is that they seem to cost a lot of money (in lunches, travel, seats at the Super Bowl) with no concrete return.

To bring us full circle, your strategic customers could also become your strategic partners, thus doubling the amount of money that could be spent on lunches.

Just as setting the right base case expectations changes management behavior and outcomes, you will be amazed how a few months of aggressive skepticism inhibit the submission of "strategic" proposals.

There are other phrases that are red flags to a cost cutter, like "core competencies" (maybe even "strategic core competencies"). It's OK to find out that you have some core competencies as a result of doing your core business for many years and it's OK to figure out how to exploit them more effectively. But if anybody proposes investing (i.e. spending lots of money with no obvious return) in building a core competence, just say no 10 times and see what happens.

The strategic skeptic also raises an eyebrow at cost lines that go down in the five-year plan but just happen to go up (as a one-off of course) in next year's annual budget. We'll get into that in more detail later.

Top Team: Finance

The chief financial officer (CFO) and the finance team must be the CEO's right hand for cost management.

The CFO provides the business with cost-management data, tools and disciplines, including core building blocks like the management accounts. No good management accounts, no chance of cost control. And the CFO should be the tough, skeptical conscience of the corporation. Challenging overblown investments and blue-sky business plans. Holding managers' backs to the wall on budgets and spending.

Many CFOs perform that role and perform it well. A minority don't. If they don't, it's usually for one of two reasons.

Some technical finance people have a poor operational understanding of the business. They have come up through the ranks as accounting, tax or treasury specialists. They know how to flow profits via tax havens and they comprehend the latest changes to GAAP on stock options. But they don't understand what drives revenue or cost, why customers buy, how the market is evolving, what drives pricing, where competitors are attacking.

For these CFOs operational results can be a complete surprise. They can put on the pinstripes and make good presentations of figures at the AGM. But they will not help you create a strong cost management culture, because fundamentally they just do not get how the business works.

I had a European client whose CFO fit this profile. He became cut off in his top-floor head office suite, surrounded by tax advisers and investment bankers pitching him complex financial engineering deals. He had no view on operational decisions and he stopped being invited to core business review meetings. Finally he got paranoid about being cut out and he resigned. His replacement had been running commercial finance for several years and so could talk to other managers as a practical line manager.

Make sure you have a CFO who understands markets, customers, competitors, pricing, operating cost. They can always hire the best tax, treasury, audit and accounting specialists under them.

A second type of finance failure is the CFO who only knows how to say no. It's no good just saying no to every investment proposal or cost increase. You have to know where and when to invest intelligently as well. The CFO needs to be an advocate of good investment as well as the champion of cost control.

I had a frustrating time with a CFO in a North American technology business. He was quite rightly pushing for a serious cost-cutting program. However, cost cutting was a necessary but not sufficient condition for turning round the business. It needed to invest at the same time, particularly in sales, like taking on one or two loss-making clients to build credibility in specific market segments. The CFO just said no to everything, so as fast as the company cut cost, sales declined even faster and it ended up worse off. (This CFO also had the first weakness, he didn't understand the operational economics.)

The best CFOs combine a real hands-on role in business strategy and operations, including knowing where and when to invest and spend, with providing strong cost-control leadership and cost-management systems.

In that context there are several central functions or departments that are key to cost control and can fit well under the CFO. I like a CFO organization that combines financial and operational roles:

❍ Technical finance
  ✳ Corporate accounts
  ✳ Audit

* Treasury
* Tax
○ Operational finance
    * Management accounts, control, planning
    * Investments – capex, mergers and acquisitions
○ Finance-related operations
    * Central procurement (of things like back-office services)
    * And maybe IT

In my experience running the organization like this is more effective than having a load of CXOs, like a chief procurement officer or a chief information officer, reporting directly to the CEO.

Top Team: Human Resources

HR is a slippery beast. In the days of my youth it was called Personnel. Now the head of Personnel has morphed into the chief talent officer.

In my time I have done my share of hating HR and they have hated me in return. Booz Allen's European personnel manager loathed me. In my short corporate life I alienated at least two HR directors – they made me play those stupid team games where you are a plant or a vegetable.

I used to hate HR because they wasted time and added cost. They spoke even more management fadbabble than consultants. Worst of all they were sanctimonious about it. "Are we reneging on our training commitments as per usual?" "The latest staff survey shows they don't feel we communicate with them." "Can we honestly say that we are a learning organization?" "We really need to invest in values, not just talk about them." (Answers: Of course! What a bunch of losers! No and we don't care. How much do you want for a team-bonding ski weekend?)

And they were the cost cutter's enemy. Whenever you raised the prospect of getting tough on people cost – doing some firings, or holding down pay rises and promotions – their knee-jerk response was to tell you all the reasons this would be a disaster for morale, productivity, future growth and so on and so on. And then why you couldn't do anything nasty anyway because of labor-protection legislation and the risk of lawsuits. It was like talking to a lawyer, not to a fellow manager.

That was in the old days. These days you can get a new breed of HR manager. She sees her job as helping you manage people cost efficiently, giving you tools to increase flexibility in dealing with staff and providing ways to manage litigation risk within a proper legal and ethical framework.

This is a revelation. Instead of being a blocker, HR becomes a core asset in the business of good cost management. Since people cost is the most strategic and difficult piece of overall cost, HR becomes a strategic partner in cost management. It takes the initiative in providing options and solutions, not barriers to action.

The BBC, which used to have a pretty cosy HR environment, has been a good example of this change. Its HR has got tough, helping to hold down excessive promotions and pay rises, demanding hard-nosed performance reviews, pushing through rounds of dead-wood pruning. No more Mister "I always wanted to work with people" Nice Guy. Impressive for a public-sector institution. (At least, it was impressive before some recent horrible reorganization efforts by the Beeb, which have just sidelined dead wood into fully paid non-jobs with no reduction in the cost structure. Tut tut, back to bad old public-sector ways, I want a license fee refund!)

If you are CEO, for cost management leadership your CFO sits at your right hand and your HR director sits at your left. You need to find an HR director who can take that position. If you are the HR director, you should want to take it.

Role Models

The CEO and the top management team should be personal role models for tight cost management.

Even when he had billions in the bank, Sam Walton used to share $50 hotel rooms with Wal-Mart regional managers when he was out on the road visiting stores. Jack Welch had a different kind of hotel room epiphany. Early in his career he found himself on the road having to share (this was GE expenses policy) a bedroom with a colleague. His takeaway was different from Sam's. He swore that when he grew up and ran GE he would make the business so successful that no manager would ever have to suffer such an indignity. In his view GE managers deserved to live a high-class life on high-class expenses.

Both people and both businesses ended up enormously successful. So which is right? Is there one good role model?

In most types of business there's only one model you can rely on and that's the frugal one. There are clear reasons a frugal role model creates value for a business and there are many successful examples.

On the other hand, while it is clearly possible to be an extravagant, high-spending leader and be very successful, that's a random outcome against the odds, like a monkey writing Shakespeare or which mutual fund does best this year. And there are so many high-profile cases where the cost excesses of bad top management role models have been leading indicators of corporate decline.

Jim Collins gives a nice illustration in *Good to Great*. He compares two steel companies, Nucor and Bethlehem Steel. Nucor had a head office of 25 staff crammed into a small rented space with cheap furniture, no reception area and catering for visitors at Phil's Diner across the street. Bethlehem Steel had a 21-story glass-and-steel head office, designed in a cross shape so lots of executives could have two-window offices, plus a fleet of corporate jets and an executive country club with its own 18-hole world-class golf course. Guess which business trounced the other in growth and profitability over several decades?

PERSONAL EXPENSES

According to BBC in-house folklore, iconic British television presenter David Attenborough is said to travel economy flying back from penguin spotting in Antarctica. One of my CEO clients carefully deducts a $10 wine from his expenses claim when we go out for a business dinner in Madrid.

These travel and entertainment behaviors set a tone that ripples down through the organization. Employees feel embarrassed about breaking with the cost culture – or at least very embarrassed about the idea of being caught. Would you be 100% comfortable if Sam Walton himself went through your hotel expenses? If other BBC presenters want to fly first, BBC finance can say but Attenborough flies economy, why can't you?

I will own up that I spent much of my working life in a very padded expenses culture. At the New York office of Booz Allen in the 1980s, if you worked past 9 p.m. you could go out and charge a meal to the client. Since most of us were workaholics with no personal life, this soon escalated from a pizza once a week to dining in one of the Zagat Top 10 every night. One evening the head of Booz New York took a client out to Lutece, then the most famous and expensive place in Manhattan, and found himself surrounded by tables of junior Booz researchers, all happily munching away at their $50-a-dish casual suppers. This unfortunately provoked a clampdown and the happy times went away; well, for a few months anyway.

Anyone who doesn't enjoy a charge-it-to-the-client juicy chateaubriand with a bottle of Vega Sicilia 91 as a young Turk on a first business trip has no soul. But any mature manager trying to build a lean, low-cost organization better be eating at Phil's Diner and picking up the tab personally.

HEAD OFFICE LOOK AND FEEL

Budget airline easyJet's corporate head office at Luton airport north of London is a construction site hut with Portaloos out back. Wal-Mart's Bentonville HQ is famously Spartan and unwelcoming, and visitors get charged for coffee. One of Scotland's wealthiest entrepreneurs has his corporate office on an old industrial estate in the rundown suburbs of Glasgow. As Derrida would say: What are these signals signifying?

If I'm a supplier, they are telling me I'd better not ask for a meeting if I'm not coming in with the best prices on the planet.

If I'm an employee out in the field actually earning money for the corporation, like running a store or down on the steel factory floor, I have to respect the head office guys for walking the talk. They're not telling me to shave to the bone and then living like fat cats themselves. That makes me more willing to go the extra mile in holding down the costs that I control. And it makes me very loyal.

An old but true analyst's joke says sell the stock when the CEO commissions a spanking new state-of-the-art corporate HQ and fills the lobby with Damien Hirst dead sheep. (In the UK, winning the Queen's Award for Industry is another sell signal.)

Head office look and feel isn't just about buildings. It's not smart to kick off a "lean organization" drive with a top management off-site at the UK's most expensive conference-and-spa hotel in the New Forest. I was there and saw it happen – the irony was lost on the CEO and we had a lot of problems on that project.

ARE THERE EXCEPTIONS?

Is this argument cheap and short-sighted? How about talent-based businesses, shouldn't they create a pampered environment to make that talent feel loved and special?

Strategy consultancies and investment banks regularly come top of the most-want-to-work-for lists of MBAs at leading business schools. The culture of these businesses is the opposite of penny pinching. It is five-star hotels, three-star restaurants, never turning right getting onto a plane, team-building weekends in Aspen and Zermatt. That tone is set from the senior partners down. And the office look and feel is prime, cut-no-corners, Park Avenue and Park Lane.

Is that a bad culture? If it isn't, doesn't that contradict the previous arguments?

The whole role model thing is more about fairness and equality than about absolute level of spending. All professional staff at McKinsey or Goldman get to share pretty equally in the same expenses lifestyle. From junior researchers up to senior partners, everybody stays in the same hotels, flies in the same class. There's no head office, all offices are equally prestigious. So the lifestyle expense is really just part of the cost of attracting and retaining the talent.

At a lower level of money, the same is true of pizza and neck massages for Silicon Valley programmers. At a higher level of money, think of personal chefs and Evian baths for movie stars.

It's different if you're running a more normal kind of business, with staff who aren't Harvard MBAs or Julia Roberts, like British Airways, Wal-Mart, the Post Office, SNCF, Coca-Cola.

COST MANAGERS: TOYOTA

Toyota is the great success story among world-scale automakers. In first quarter 2007 it overtook GM as the world's largest vehicle manufacturer. Over the last decade it has grown volume at 7% a year compound, vs 1.5% at GM. Over the same period it had more than double the profits of GM and Ford combined, with nobody else anywhere in sight.

Toyota's success comes partly from branding, design, innovation and quality. Its top-end Lexus brand is built on a culture of near-perfection – the separation between hood and grille on each model can't be greater than an eyelash. The result: Lexus has soundly beaten both Mercedes and BMW in the US luxury car market.

But it also comes from a deep and sophisticated drive for cost management. In the Toyota culture this is known as the drive to eliminate waste, a core theme of the business underpinning the formidable Toyota Production System.

Fujio Cho, president since 1999, says that Toyota starts with two questions:

O Where are we wasting resources like time, people or material?
O How can we be less wasteful?

He takes the example of conveyor belts: "Some manufacturers use them to move a product from worker to worker on an assembly line. But belts can actually waste time because workers have to take the product off the belt at each manufacturing step. It's faster to keep the component stationary and have workers approach it as necessary."

This kill-waste culture is now deeply embedded, from top managers down to factory-floor employees. It provides the base platform of efficiency onto which the company can lay the super-values of invention, aspiration and perfection.

Toolkit – Cost Leadership

A CHALLENGING BASE CASE
O Is your base case for annual budgets and cost reviews always a challenging one?
O Are you constantly pushing the organization to be more cost efficient – and this year not next year?

○ Have your direct reports learnt to expect that, so they no longer bother coming in with anything less aggressive?

INDIVIDUAL ACCOUNTABILITY
○ Is it absolutely clear which individual manager is 100% responsible for hitting which cost targets?
○ Have you eliminated joint or fuzzy accountabilities?

PERSISTENCE
○ Does the organization believe 100% that you will always persist in the drive for cost efficiencies?
○ That you won't ever forget commitments or let targets drift?
○ That you won't be deflected with fudges, half measures, long timetables?

CONTINUOUS IMPROVEMENT
○ Do you have a CI culture?

SHORT TIMEFRAMES
○ Do you work on short-term targets, asking for concrete progress to be made this week, this month?

FEEDBACK LOOPS
○ Is there a process for seeing quickly and clearly what progress is being made on cost targets?
○ Does the process involve good hard data, delivered quickly, reviewed frequently, with visibility and transparency?

STRATEGIC SKEPTICISM
○ Are your managers very nervous about coming in with proposals to invest in "strategic partnerships" or "core competencies"?

TOP TEAM

○ Is there a strong CFO and finance function as the CEO's critical right hand for cost management?

○ And a proactive hard-nosed HR function, willing to take the lead in managing the key issues of people cost and staff productivity?

ROLE MODELS

○ Are you and your top managers good role models in terms of personal expense habits?

○ Is there fairness or equality in expense policies and behavior down through the organization?

○ Have you created a head office environment and style that send the right cost message to suppliers and employees?

3

Techniques and Tactics

B efore we take a look at how cost leadership can be applied in particular areas and functions, here are some overall techniques and tactics for getting the best results. I've used all of them over the years, on dozens of consulting projects and as a CFO.

Understanding Cost Dynamics

I would not say that the future is necessarily less predictable than the past. I think the past was not predictable when it started.

—Donald Rumsfeld

First, you need to understand cost drivers and cost dynamics. What creates cost? How do costs move? In particular:

○ Which costs move mainly with revenue and how?
○ Which costs move mainly with headcount and how?
○ What are the main drivers of all other remaining big lumps of cost?
○ What are the key cost trends, up and down?

Take a headcount hiring decision. Direct salary and bonus cost might be $50,000. Add in payroll taxes and benefits like healthcare or a car. Then include other fully variable costs (which would not exist if that person wasn't on the payroll) like a mobile phone, travel and entertainment (T&E) for a salesperson, personal computer gear. $50,000 has become $80,000. Now you know how costs really change with changes in headcount.

A key metric to track is people-related cost (PRC) by department and level.

Business ABC
Department XYZ

	Q1	Q2	Q3	Q4
PRC, $000				
Payroll	4000	4120	4244	4371
Tax and benefits	800	906	1018	1136
T&E	150	180	216	259
Personal comms	200	200	200	200
Personal IT	200	180	162	146
Total PRC	5350	5586	5840	6112
Average headcount	200	204	208	212
PRC/head, annualized	107	110	112	115
% change, annualized		9.5	10.0	10.4

In the example you can see that total PRC per head is increasing at a 10% annual rate, which is pretty high. Your team is going to get very expensive unless you can change the trend. The fastest increase is in taxes and benefits, so you could focus there.

This type of calculation doesn't capture all the costs of headcount, however. If you hire lots of extra people, you might have to rent extra office space and hire additional managers and support staff in accounting and HR. These are step-change costs. For day-to-day management you keep these separate from the fully variable costs. You have to know what they are, but they don't change so much so often and they usually involve a different set of decisions.

Headcount cost is one of the three key *cost creators* that drive cost dynamics:

○ **Revenue producing** – the cost created by a production unit or a service activity, or by a customer or transaction.
○ **Headcount** – as just discussed.
○ **Others** – cost created by having a facility or a location, or by an enterprise process.

Take an airline's cost structure. An airline's key production unit is a flight. Many costs occur if and when a plane goes from A to B: fuel, pilots and cabin crew, aircraft depreciation and maintenance, take-off and landing charges, air traffic control.

Some costs come from having an individual passenger: in-flight meals, sales (bookings, changes, refunds), airport handling (check-in, baggage, airport passenger charges).

Other costs are driven by choice of home base and hub airports. For British Airways, flying out of Heathrow costs a lot more than flying out of Gatwick. BA's low-cost competitors use cheaper London airports, Stansted and Luton. If an airline flies between Poland and the UK, its labor cost will be a lot lower if it can use Poland-based pilots and cabin crew and overnight them in the UK as necessary rather than vice versa.

Finally, there are costs associated with central enterprise processes like brand building (advertising, Airmiles, PR, loyalty programs); safety and regulatory compliance; inventory and yield management; or financial control and compliance.

Once you have broken down the costs accurately in this way and understood the drivers and dynamics, you can:

○ Work on driving down unit cost in each area.
○ Accurately model and manage costs and financial outcomes, including what happens if volume changes from budget/plan.
○ Price accurately, so as not to lose money unintentionally on sales and to stimulate "win–win" behavior from customers.

Not understanding cost drivers and cost dynamics is very dangerous. I once worked in the US with a software business at an early stage of development. The founder CEO had come from Microsoft. His mental model of software economics was the Microsoft model for Windows and Office: high up-front development and mass marketing cost, then very low variable production, delivery and service cost on each new customer and sale. So each additional sale carried a very high 90% profit margin. The key unit of cost for Windows or Office was developing the product suite; after that the cost per customer was very low.

The CEO's new business was selling CRM software licenses to medium-size companies. Sales were starting to take off but the expected profitability wasn't flowing through as sales volume built up. The CEO was expecting the 90% marginal profitability on new sales that he was familiar with at Microsoft.

But selling enterprise software to medium-size companies just wasn't like that. A load of extra cost was required on every additional sale: very expensive in-person sales meetings, sales commissions, OEM software purchases, product customization and demos, professional services for installation and training.

It turned out that the key unit of cost for this business was the cost to sell and service an individual customer. That cost was running at over 60% of sales value. The marginal profitability of an additional sale was maybe 30%, not Microsoft's 90%.

We had to get more aggressive on pricing and focus on how to drive down our sales and service cost per customer, including charging for professional services that we had been giving away free or at below cost. We also had to rethink our financial plans and how much cash we needed before we got to breakeven.

As another example, I was working with one of the top internet-only travel agencies. They had built a good sales base and were pushing toward profitability. Each additional transaction needed to be profit positive, at least covering its variable cost.

Like traditional travel agencies they considered variable cost to be only "fulfillment cost": call center, tickets, credit card charges. But for internet retailers this was no longer true. Marketing had become mainly a variable cost. Extra transactions generally involved paying for keywords, search engine ads, shopbot and affiliate commissions. These variable online marketing costs were bigger per transaction than fulfillment cost. For low-margin products like hotel and short-haul air they made extra transactions loss making – so the more the revenue, the greater the losses.

Once this was understood, the business made certain it was spending online marketing money only where it generated a positive marginal contribution.

Management Accounts and Metrics

Oh! Blessed rage for order, pale Ramon.

—Wallace Stevens

A good set of management accounts is the single most important tool for cost management. It should read like a Walter Mosley novel or a David Hockney painting. Elegantly structured and crisply presented. Telling a deep and complex story in a few concise lines. With character and characters, narrative and mood. It should show an artist, the CFO, at the height of his or her powers.

A bad set of management accounts is a reliable indicator that a business is being poorly managed.

You need management accounts that:

○ Tell a rich story of what is happening with the business economics – history, today, future projections.
○ Allow you to see what is going right and what is going wrong, and so where you need to take action.

○ Let you model outcomes under different scenarios.
○ Track progress against plans and targets, in ways that reinforce lead manager accountability.
○ Do all this in an accurate, insightful and time-efficient way.

Management accounts should not be confused with other sets of accounts for corporate and tax reporting. Management accounts are internal operating tools for the CFO, the CEO and all line managers.

I like a one-page (one spreadsheet page) format that takes the P&L down to operating profit before interest and tax, runs through operating cash flow, and adds in underneath a selection of key operating statistics and metrics. I also like a quarterly presentation over a two-year period, with actuals for last year and budget vs actuals for the current year as the core format.

MANAGEMENT ACCOUNTS FORMAT

		Quarters – last year Actual	Quarters – this year Budget & actual	Sum financial year Last Current (B&A)
Revenue	... ...			
Cost	... ...			
Operating profit				
Add depreciation Deduct capex Change in WC Operating cash flow				

Key operating statistics & metrics
  Headcount ...
  Direct cost/head ...				

If you limit yourself to only a dozen or so cost lines to play with, you have to decide what information you need most. My order of priority is:

1 Identify non-headcount costs that are or should be driven by revenue and that move very closely with revenue – cost of goods sold (COGS) or variable costs.
2 Identify all other costs that are driven by in-house staff headcount (payroll, benefits, T&E).
3 That leaves a bunch of all other costs that are not driven, in the short term, by revenue or headcount – like facilities, external services, marketing, IT and communications, contractors and outsourcing.
4 Report costs in buckets that align as much as possible with lead manager accountability.

So the previous format could be fleshed out like this.

MANAGEMENT ACCOUNTS FORMAT, WITH DETAIL					
$M		Manager lead	Period Q1	Q2	
Revenue		Sales	25.4	31.0	
COGS		Engineering	-4.9	-6.6	
Gross profit			20.5	24.4	
Heads cost	Sales	Sales	-8.1	-9.0	
	Engineering	Engineering	-7.4	-7.2	
	G&A	Finance	-3.4	-3.5	
Other cost	Facilities	Finance	-2.0	-2.0	
	Marketing	Sales	-1.1	-1.5	
	Prof. services	Finance	-0.5	-0.2	
Operating profit			-2.0	1.0	
Key operating statistics & metrics					
Revenue growth, % Q on Q				22%	
% of revenue	COGS		19.3%	21.3%	
	Sales heads cost		-31.9%	-29.0%	
Engineering	Heads #		200	180	
	Annualized cost per head $000		148	160	
...	...				

This lets me see quickly that:

○ COGS is 20% of revenue – every dollar we sell converts into 80 cents of gross profit, to pay for all our fixed and semi-fixed costs.
○ Headcount cost accounts for the vast majority of all our other costs; engineering cost per head is growing fast and is shown as a key metric.

○ All the cost buckets are clearly assigned to one lead manager.

There are many other different ways in which you could aggregate and present costs in the management accounts. You may need to drop to the next level of functional or departmental detail, like breaking out sales into new business, account management, support and marketing. If you had multiple business units you would report business unit contribution and then some shared central costs. You might footnote the accounts with summary natural cost categories: power, telecoms, payroll taxes.

The goal is a set of operating accounts that lets you understand, model and manage the true economics of your business.

Bang for Buck

You should focus most cost management attention and effort on where you can get the biggest results fast.

I could call this the ABC approach. If you were to list all possible cost-reduction opportunities in order of potential impact, you would have some As with big impact, some Bs with medium impact, and a long tail of Cs where each idea doesn't count for much. (Just to be clear, "ABC" here does not refer to Activity-Based Costing.)

Or you might see it as illustrating the 80:20 principle: 80% of cost opportunity comes from the best 20% of ideas. This is one of those blindingly obvious things that people know but ignore. They carry on spending 80% of their time on the things that matter least. In their head they are clearing the ground for an attack on the big stuff, but somehow that never happens.

To make sure I follow an ABC or 80:20 approach, I put all my possible cost action programs into a simple matrix, illustrated opposite. Across the top of the matrix I estimate the potential cost impact, the expected value of future cost savings over a five- or ten-year

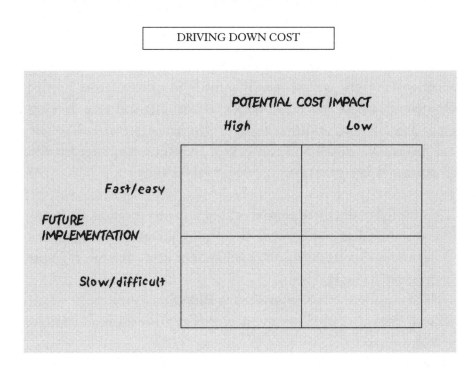

period, ignoring the practicalities of implementation. Down the side of the matrix I add in the question of practicality. Can I get the savings quickly and easily? Or will I have to work away at them for years, tackling difficult obstacles: internal politics, labor laws, government regulation, joint-venture partners, long-term contracts.

The matrix helps clarify which ideas to pursue first and hard and which ones to put on the back burner:

- ○ In the top left are the #1 priorities, the no-brainers: big cost benefits, quick and straightforward to implement.
- ○ I then move to the top right for my #2 priorities: maybe not such big opportunities but quick results.
- ○ Then I move to the bottom left: big opportunities, but ones where you could bash your head against a brick wall for a long time, so the strategy is to work away quietly and steadily at removing obstacles.
- ○ Finally, any ideas that fall into the bottom right get put aside on a very slow back burner – you only start on them if there's really nothing else left to do.

I had an IT client with three different head offices across Europe. One handled data and network operations, one software development and support, and one all the commercial activities like sales and finance. We developed a list of cost-reduction options, each with an estimated five-year savings value, total $250m:

○ Consolidate the three central offices into one location, $50m.
○ Outsource data and network operations, $60m.
○ Take some percentage of development and support offshore, probably to India, $50m.
○ Take out some layers in marketing and sales, $10m.
○ Shift network purchases to a lower-cost pan-European contract, $20m.
○ Cut travel cost, $10m.
○ Change front-end development processes to reduce back-end cost (bug fixes, reinstalls, customer support), $50m.

Looking down the list we had four big-impact ($50–60m) and three low-impact ($10–20m) ideas.

Two of our four big ideas were quite straightforward to execute. Outsourcing operations had been gaining management acceptance and there were three credible suppliers waiting to bid. Offshoring development to India was still controversial, but other firms had done it and we were proposing a cautious, step-by-step approach.

The two other big-impact ideas were much trickier to implement. Changing the front-end development process was fine and elegant on paper. But it was a complicated change, we wouldn't see benefits for over a year or maybe two, and there were big internal arguments about how to do it. We decided to keep working away at it but not include it in this year's cost-reduction plans.

Consolidating the three main offices was a no-brainer operationally but horrible politically. Each of three main shareholders represented a country where one of the offices was based. The company had to deal with state subsidies and public-sector customers, who would put pressure on to keep local offices open. Labor-protection laws were tough. Top management didn't have the stomach for big office closures and firings. We could go on about the size of the prize, but nothing was going to happen.

Out of the three low-impact ideas, two were quick and easy: negotiate a better pan-European network contract and cut travel spend. The third involved cutting out layers between customers, country distributors, regional sales and marketing teams and central marketing. A good idea, but there was no consensus on which layers to take out, the cost savings weren't huge and there was some sales risk.

In the end our matrix looked like the one below.

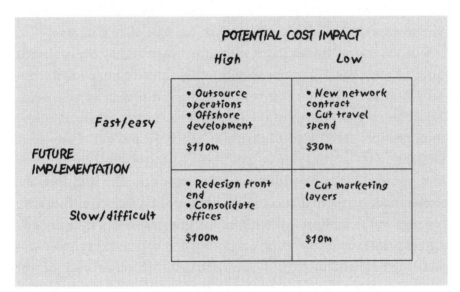

	POTENTIAL COST IMPACT	
	High	Low
Fast/easy	• Outsource operations • Offshore development $110m	• New network contract • Cut travel spend $30m
Slow/difficult	• Redesign front end • Consolidate offices $100m	• Cut marketing layers $10m

FUTURE IMPLEMENTATION

We could get $140m of the $250m quite quickly and easily. We started working away on the two big-impact but hard-to-do ideas, working toward a future $100m saving. And we dumped the idea of cutting marketing layers.

When you do this kind of analysis, make sure you identify the key choices correctly. In the case above we had lots of minor options for cutting operations cost while still keeping it in-house. If we had pursued that logic we would have missed the big cost-cutting option, outsourcing the whole activity.

Slice and Dice

You can attack difficult areas of cost by slicing and dicing.

Say your business provides financial advice and services to high net worth individuals (HNWIs) via multiple channels: a branch network, one-on-one visits to clients, the phone and the internet. It's a profitable business, but the sales and service cost is very high and has resisted all efforts to increase productivity. Your sales team insists that a wealthy individual always requires personal one-on-one human contact. You don't want to risk any loss of customers.

But the broad umbrella of customer interaction covers a wide range of activities. For some activities high-quality, high-touch contact is valuable; for others it isn't. For some it may even be a negative, requiring too much of their time. The customer base also isn't homogenous: some HNWIs have assets of $5 million, some have $100,000.

If you put these two ideas together, you can slice and dice the problem and get a reduction in cost without risking customer loss. For high-value interactions with high-value customers (like reviewing a portfolio or introducing new products) you could keep a high-cost, high-touch, in-person approach. At the other end of the spectrum, lower-value interactions (like portfolio valuation updates or annual tax statements) with lower-value customers, you could switch to low-cost types of contact like email and the internet. Graphically that strategy could look like the matrix opposite.

Or take an example from the software industry. You have a development team in the San Francisco Bay Area or in the UK's Thames Valley. Total cost per developer is $150,000, very expensive. You want to reduce the cost by going offshore to India, where cost

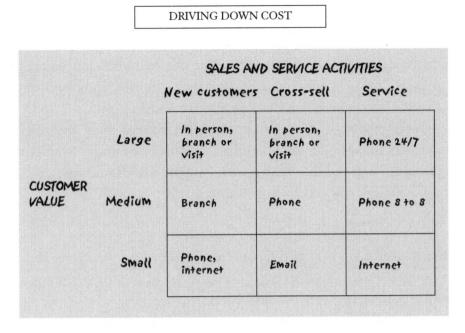

	SALES AND SERVICE ACTIVITIES		
	New customers	Cross-sell	Service
Large	In person, branch or visit	In person, branch or visit	Phone 24/7
CUSTOMER VALUE **Medium**	Branch	Phone	Phone 8 to 8
Small	Phone, internet	Email	Internet

per developer, even after extra overhead and communications, is well under $50,000.

But your head of development is very uncomfortable with that idea. While she knows other software and IT businesses are going offshore, she's worried that the team's knowledge won't transfer to India, quality will suffer, product will ship late, bugs will multiply – and she'll get blamed.

The answer is to slice and dice the problem. Trying out offshore development will be less risky if you can try it first with specific sub-tasks that are:

○ Remote from the end customer.
○ Not on the critical path for product delivery.
○ Based on common, well-understood technical skills.
○ Not dependent on heavy, frequent interaction with a core head office team.

This cut might convince her to try out offshoring on activities like reversioning, version.dot updates and fixes, testing, database maintenance, technical support. Once she sees it can deliver good quality at lower cost, it can get rolled out to more complex and business-critical functions. (In fact, major software firms from the US and Europe have already started to use India for product R&D.)

Core activities, like product development and sales, are often treated as monolithic wholes and allowed to be immune from cost cutting. Slicing and dicing lets you overcome that immunity, step by step, with low risk.

Understanding Natural Cost Trends

Be like water making its way through cracks…
If nothing within you stays rigid, outward things will disclose themselves.
—Bruce Lee

Without you doing anything about it, some costs naturally go up and some naturally go down.

You might think you're doing really well at managing costs, but in fact you're just pushing water downhill since the natural trend is down. You're paying bonuses to managers who actually could have cut much deeper. Competitors are cutting harder and faster than you. They are building future price reductions into their competitive quotes and you can't figure out how they can bid that low and make money.

Or you might think you can keep costs down in the future when in fact there's no chance of doing that – the natural trend is up. You are giving your customers long-term pricing contracts on that basis, locking in future losses. You are wasting time in tense budget meetings with managers who can't reverse a nasty cost trend.

Let's look at some costs that tend to go down. Take communications. The marginal cost of an extra phone call or data packet is close to zero. Technology cost is declining. There is huge global over-capacity. Barriers around national markets are vanishing. Internet

communication is virtually free. No wonder comms costs are collapsing. So when your head of network operations comes into the
annual budget session looking smug with a next-year cut of –3%,
your only question is why not –30%? (And let's *not* lock in that
three-year pricing contract with Sprint.)

Or take manufactured goods. China makes everything 10%
cheaper every year. Physical distribution, from Asia to Europe and
North America, is more efficient. Trade barriers have come down.
Dell's entry-level laptop now costs $600 versus over $1,500 five
years ago. Tesco in the UK has a DVD player at the equivalent of $50
versus $500 five years ago. So don't sign that three-year leasing con-
tract for PCs – you'll gain a bit of cash flow but pay double the real
cost over three years.

Some other costs tend to go up. Only one category really matters:
people cost. The cost of a person generally goes up at 1–2% faster
than inflation. You had better be getting productivity growth –
higher output or lower headcount – or your unit costs are increasing
more and more. On the people cost treadmill you have to run hard
just to stay still.

I was working with a US technology business in 2004. The business had had a hard time since Y2K and 9/11. We had cut the cost
base (meaning mainly the headcount, which was 80% of cost) and
clawed back to a not-bad 10% profit margin. Now the CEO was saying she had to take a breather, stop cutting, the organization had to
have a period of stability. Our problem was that we were projecting
flat revenue and she was assuming that existing staff wages would
grow at 4% a year. In three years we would be back down to
breakeven. We had no choice but to keep on cutting at least 4% of
the headcount every year, for as far ahead as we could see, just to
hold profits flat.

In some cases the natural cost trend is worse than that. Bangalore
is the epicenter of the explosion in Indian offshore IT. Average IT
salaries in Bangalore are growing at 15–20% a year; for specialists or

experienced managers the growth rate can be 30%. Clearly this won't go on for ever, as in five or ten years a developer in Bangalore would then cost the same as one in Seattle. But even for a few years this creates a huge headache around pricing, recruiting and cost planning.

Outside services can also shoot up in price. For example, when you combine cost escalation in property services with a labor skills shortage, you get the London phenomenon of £150 ($300) call-out plumbers (followed by a mass immigration of plumbers from Poland).

In the West, services needing local labor keep going up in cost, while products that can be manufactured in volume in China go down in cost dramatically. You can see that effect in these UK retail price trends over the last ten years:

O Audiovisual goods (televisions, stereos, DVDs etc.)
  ✴ Cost of product: – 50%
  ✴ Cost of repair: + 50%
O Clothes
  ✴ Cost of product: – 60%
  ✴ Cleaning, repair, hire: + 34%

Which is why we no longer fix televisions or mend trousers, we just buy new ones.

Cash Cost not P&L Cost

Cash cost is what matters, not what you might show as cost on the profit and loss statement.

For non-accountants, the difference between cash and P&L cost relates to things that you capitalize and then depreciate over more than a year, like equipment, vehicles, fit-out costs for property, IP licenses. If I buy a computer for $3,000 cash cost today but I think it has a useful life of three years, I capitalize the cost, then every year for three years take a $1,000 charge on the P&L.

In some businesses this difference is not a big deal. In advertising or accounting very little stuff gets capitalized. But in some businesses these capital expenditures may be the biggest cost items – when you are building a base station network for mobile phones or drilling for oil in Kazakhstan, for instance.

To be a good cost manager you need to intercept cost before it occurs. It's no good looking at a cost line showing a $200,000 "spend" on office fixtures and fittings and shouting at the department head that it's too high, when the cash spend occurred two years ago and the depreciation is just rolling through the P&L.

You have to capture and control the cash cost at the point of decision making, at the point of actual spend. In any crisis cost-reduction program you switch all the short-term management accounts onto a cash basis. You then reconcile that back to the normal P&L presentation to avoid hours debating what the numbers mean.

Illustration of cash cost reporting

	Q1 Actual	Q2 LE	Q3 Budget	Q4 Budget
Normal reported P&L cost	100	98	96	94
Take out depreciation	-30	-26	-22	-18
Op cost excluding capex	70	73	74	76
Add in capex	35	40	35	40
Cash costs	105	113	109	116

In this example the cash cost trend is very different from the P&L cost trend. P&L cost is going down, from 100 to 94, which sounds like good news. But that's entirely due to lower depreciation, stuff we bought years ago reaching the end of its accounting life. When we take out depreciation we can see the other operating costs going up from 70 to 76, so clearly we haven't got a grip on them yet. Then when we add in the capex it's a horror – we're spending much more on capex than our depreciation charge, and total cash cost is going up from 105 to 116. Those capex decisions will be hostages to fortune as they flow through the P&L over the next several years, so we need to clamp down now.

At the peak of the dot-com and telco bubble of 2000, investment bankers were looking for ways to justify ridiculous business valuations. One measure of business value is the price-to-earnings ratio: if a company is worth $100m and its earnings (profits) are $5m, it has a P/E ratio of 20. In the year 2000 P/E ratios, calculated on a normal basis, were looking insane, higher than ever before in stock market history.

So bankers came up with a new way of calculating profits, to make the profits higher and the P/E ratio lower. The new way was EBITDA: Earnings Before Interest, Tax, Depreciation and Amortization. OK, it is sensible to take out interest, tax and amortization, but taking out depreciation is just absurd. Telco executives couldn't believe their luck and started chucking bucketloads of capex at their businesses, building huge excess capacity in global phone networks. Then the bubble burst and people realized: hey, cost is cost after all, even if you spread it in the books over future generations.

I tried patenting my own variations on EBITDA, like EBAPTA: Earnings Before Any Payments To Anybody. My favorite was simply R: Revenue. I couldn't get Merrill or Goldman interested in buying the intellectual property, unfortunately.

Best Practice (and Level Playing Fields)

If you have lots of units doing similar things, you have a great cost management opportunity. You can look for best practice.

Let's say you run a chain of 20 fashion stores. You set central standards for staffing ratios, merchandising, customer satisfaction, sales productivity and so on, and you tell store managers to run the shops to those standards. But still you find there are big differences in productivity. Some managers will be better than others at finding more efficient ways to do things. Some will simply run things tighter. If you can identify these shops and what they're doing better, you can apply their best practices to the whole chain.

This is a better way of showing how far you can drive cost efficiency than anything you could produce via head office analysis or diktat. It has come from the field. It's the result of lots of micro decisions, changes, innovations and outcomes, as well as lots of micro competition.

To tease out best practice you still need to do some work, though. You have to put everybody on a level playing field before you can draw any conclusions.

Say you're trying to find out which store has the most productive staff, measured by sales per staff-person day. On first analysis, say Store 9 looks like the winner, with sales per staff day of $1,000.

However, you're not yet looking at a level playing field. The bigger the overall sales per store, the easier it is to schedule staff efficiently and the less overhead staff you need per salesperson. So you'd expect larger stores to have better productivity.

Digging deeper, you now see that Store 9 is one of your largest stores and is actually less productive than you would expect given its overall sales volume. Your real best practice model is quite a small store, say Store 17, even though its sales per staff day are only $800, because it punches way above its expected weight. If you hadn't leveled the playing field you would have reached the wrong conclusions.

Now you need to find out how Store 17 is getting that productivity. You need to talk to the manager and staff and observe the store in action, and do the same with a control group of less-productive stores.

You can apply this approach to sales offices and sales teams, contact centers, factories, field service engineers, overhead costs in different business units.

My wife works in the BBC's Science department, producing documentaries. The beauty of working in a big organization with a big output – in this case, the biggest in the world in its genre – is that you get to see a large sample of different approaches to what you are doing. Which programs came in over or under cost budget, for what reasons? Which programs delivered best bang for buck in audience share and critical reviews? Which mix of cost between pre-production, in-production and post-production delivered best value for money?

Best practice works well when your database is internal. If anybody challenges the analysis you have 100% access to the real data to prove things one way or another.

Applying best practice externally, across a peer group of competitors, is more problematic. Consultants sell these studies as competitive best practice or competitive benchmarking projects. I have never seen a great result. Most review meetings are spent discussing why such and such a number can't be comparable or working out that competitors are defining things completely differently. Net result: no action programs and a report filed away as "interesting, must update it next year".

One time you can really do a competitive benchmarking is when you've just acquired or merged with a competitor in the same business. Now you have full open access and you can make sure you compare apples to apples. This is a great opportunity: the two businesses will have taken different approaches to several activities and now is the chance to find out which are more efficient. Seize the chance quickly – soon the organizations get merged and the differences get lost.

Competitive Analysis

Although it is hard to do useful competitive benchmarking, some forms of competitive analysis are useful for cost management. Their main value lies in addressing structural cost issues rather than in attempting to do detailed operational benchmarking.

For example, I once worked with a major European airline, an old-style full-cost carrier, which needed to convince its unions of the need for changes in staffing levels, working practices and pay rates. We were able to give analytical proof that most competitors had been managing to reduce their overall unit operating cost steadily over the previous 10 years, while my client had only managed to hold unit costs flat. We could also demonstrate the structural cost advantage (in productivity and in pay) enjoyed by new competitors: low-cost carriers on short haul and Asian carriers on long haul. In both cases the absolute accuracy of the analysis was not the issue and could be argued, but the general direction and conclusion could not be, which finally opened up useful union discussion and changes in the labor agreements.

Competitive analysis can also help separate structural cost differences from operational execution and reveal new opportunities. For example, an American client was very proud of having a service-cost-to-sales ratio that was much better than its competitors. But digging into the data, this cost ratio was closely related to geographical customer density and average customer size. On both measures my client had a big advantage over competitors. This was good for profitability but not for cost efficiency – once those structural differences were adjusted for, my client was actually much higher cost than it should have been and we initiated a cost-reduction program. We would never have arrived at that opportunity without competitive analysis.

Toolkit – Techniques and Tactics

COST DYNAMICS
O Understand what creates cost.
O And what your key cost trends are.
O And how costs move in relation to decisions and activities, in particular how they move with revenue and headcount.

MANAGEMENT ACCOUNTS
O Produce management accounts that let you understand, model and manage the true economics of the business.
O Is the presentation as crisp as Elmore Leonard's dialogue?

BANG FOR BUCK
O Focus on where to get the biggest results fastest.

SLICE AND DICE
O Get at difficult costs by slicing and dicing.
O Unbundle activities.
O Map them against different customer segments.

PUSHING WATER DOWNHILL
O Understand natural cost trends.
O Don't fool yourself you are pushing water downhill.
O Don't expect to push water uphill.

FOCUS ON CASH COST NOT P&L COST
O Particularly in a cash crunch.

BEST PRACTICE
O Regularly look for best practice across the organization.
O Take opportunities to do experiments and comparisons.

COMPETITIVE ANALYSIS

O Check competitors' cost positions and their cost trend. Have they found more cost-effective ways of working?

O Make sure you distinguish structural cost differences from operational execution.

4

People

Girls take this tip from me
Get a working man when you marry
And let all those sweet men be

—Bessie Smith

The cost of people, of full-time staff, is the most difficult cost to manage. Because it is so tricky it is usually left until last in any cost-cutting program and any discussion of cost management. Let's reverse that trend and look at it now before we go on to easier tasks, like dealing with suppliers.

Why Is People Cost so Problematic?

First, people cost is very sticky. Once people are on the payroll it's hard to get them off, even if they are poor performers. There's a natural momentum the other way: to give them raises and promotions, to provide extra staff under them to help out.

Nobody likes being the bad guy who has to fire people, refuse a promotion, tell staff how they're underperforming. Everybody wants to avoid those conversations – why can't we give it another year to see if there's an improvement or can somebody else deal with it please?

In the West there is tough legal protection of employees. Cutting staff can be slow or impossible as well as very expensive. A company, or an individual manager, can be sued for discrimination or unfair process if things go wrong. And even if a business is collapsing it is rare for staff to accept any cuts in pay.

Secondly, people form the main area of cost that goes up relentlessly in real terms. Wages in Europe and North America increase over the long run at 1-2% a year faster than inflation. This is productivity growth, good for the economy and good for personal wealth. But it is an ongoing cost challenge for any people business.

In service businesses people cost is by far the majority of total cost. In North America and Europe services now account for over two-thirds of the economy, replacing agriculture and manufacturing. Managing payroll has therefore become the biggest cost issue.

Thirdly, real people cost is a lot larger than it seems. People create indirect costs other than payroll, like facilities, equipment and travel. Adding headcount in production or sales means more overhead staff in HR and accounting.

The full long-term cost of staff may not show up on today's accounts. Employee stock options dilute future value for shareholders. Unfunded pension liabilities amount to over half of market capitalization at several Global 500 companies. Under bizarre government accounting rules the UK public sector does not have to account at all for huge future pension obligations – if it did, its payroll would look 15-20% higher. The British government has an unfunded pension gap of at least £700 billion ($1.3 trillion), over half annual GDP, and this number gets much bigger every time someone gets around to recalculating it.

Fourthly, headcount tends to multiply like an out-of-control chain reaction. You hire one person, then you find out three months later that the first thing she's done is hire a department around her.

Take software sales. You hire a senior sales guy and expect (reasonably enough) that he might actually make some sales calls. No. He spends his first three months sitting at his desk developing a sales team hiring plan (and a sales comp model). He tells you that's his first priority – how can he sell anything when he's got no team to support him? So you give him the benefit of the doubt and say OK, you can hire two junior sales guys to give you leverage. They get hired and what do they do in their first three months? You guessed it. And you're stuck in a sort of existential sales management hell, where no sales calls ever get made but the sales force doubles every quarter.

For all these reasons, getting a tough handle on people cost is critical.

Hiring

Why are you hiring? Do you really need an extra person? If you nip unnecessary hiring in the bud you'll save yourself a lot of pain later.

Are you hiring another person to do an existing job because the workload has grown? Find ways to get more productive with the staff you have. Stay with that approach for a long time before you give up on it.

Or are you hiring a new person for a new job? Make sure you have a real justification for that new activity, a proper investment case.

HUMAN CAPITAL...IZATION

A good trick for getting a grip on headcount growth is to treat all hiring decisions as capital investments. Capitalize their likely future cost, then evaluate the hiring decision just like you would a major investment in a production line or a multimillion-dollar IT project.

Say you are thinking of hiring a junior marketing executive. You've got the candidate, she's been freelancing with you for several months and she wants to come in as full-time in-house staff.

The decision doesn't look very expensive. She already costs you $1,000 a week as a freelance. On payroll she'll come in at 20% less than that, although there'll be pension, benefits and payroll taxes on top. Let's say total annual cost is comparable, around $50,000. This is easily within your annual budget approval levels and it doesn't look like a big decision.

It does if you capitalize it.

What if she doesn't work out? You might know from experience that nobody gets fired in less than three years no matter how bad they are – and then only if they're really bad or they misbehave. It might take two or three years just to arrive at a balanced fair view; then a year of indecision and prevarication; then a year of warnings and HR due processes. In practice it might take five years to reverse the hire – and at the end you'll also pay six months' severance.

So this hiring decision really is a commitment to five or six years of cost even if it doesn't work out. The real cost of that decision might be more like five times the annual cost – $250,000 rather than $50,000. Now you're going to be much more cautious. You might even take it before an investment committee.

In the public sector there is much less incentive for managers to reverse bad hiring decisions. Bad hires stay in the system for longer, or for ever, maybe getting shuffled sideways so a new manager has to deal with the problem. Employees are also voters, so politicians meddle in job protection. People cost here is even stickier than in the private sector.

In recent years in the UK you could have got paranoid about future tax levels if you looked at the *Guardian* newspaper's midweek "Society" insert, the UK public sector's largest jobs board. The pages of classified recruitment ads multiplied like rabbits after the 2001 election, when then Chancellor Gordon Brown opened the taps on government spending. You could have been tempted by a job as Household Refuse Strategy Officer in a London borough on £75,000 ($150,000) a year. Or Change Manager for Community Diversity in mid Wales on £60,000 ($120,000) a year. Happy times were very much here again for British public-sector hiring and that headcount isn't going to go away in a hurry. And of course all the jobs came with final-salary pensions, which the private sector can no longer afford.

In some continental European countries employment regulation makes it very hard to fire people. In Belgium it is in practice close to impossible. In Spain severance costs can be so high they effectively rule out any firings. If you combine these two factors – public-sector jobs in countries with high employment protection – you could argue for a capitalization multiple of 15 to 20 times. How often do Italian civil servants get fired? One low-level clerk on $30,000 a year ends up being a $500,000 taxpayer investment.

In the 1970s ad agencies used to say: "This is a great business, but the assets go down in the elevator at night." This was said with regret that the human assets were so mobile and hard to lock down. Unfortunately it is also true that the human liabilities take the elevator back up the next morning.

Get a grip on hiring fever. Capitalize, capitalize, capitalize.

MINIMUM RISK, MAXIMUM FLEXIBILITY

When you do hire, try to use more short-term contracts and part-time staff.

There are obvious benefits for employers: fewer employment liabilities, a more variable cost structure, lower indirect costs.

And there are benefits for employees too. Being able to work part-time with flexible hours opens up job options to mothers and retirees. Working short-term contracts suits mobile professionals like programmers or designers. The internet and declining telecom costs make it possible to do many jobs from remote or home locations. These are win–wins for employers and staff alike.

Paying

In the province of New York… ship carpenters earn ten shillings and sixpence a day, with a pint of rum worth sixpence sterling.

—Adam Smith, *The Wealth of Nations*

Once people are on the payroll the natural momentum of raises and promotions takes over. One tedious but unavoidable job you have as a manager is fending off endless moans from your staff that they are undervalued/underpaid/underpromoted. (Although your own moans to your boss are of course totally justified.)

There's no magic bullet for dealing with this, it's just a fact of life. But it soon gets round the organization if you're a soft touch and give in quickly. Always take at least three months to think about it. Never say "probably", that gets heard as "yes".

You should also assume that every pay and promotion decision is public. You may want to do a quiet deal with a top talent who's threatening to leave, but it probably won't stay private for long. You've just set a big precedent. Next week there'll be a line of people outside your office demanding to know why they don't deserve the same.

SALARY SURVEYS AND TOP QUARTILES

Managers fed up with being pestered on pay might commission a salary survey. They are looking for an objective external measure of what is reasonable pay so the issue can be put to bed.

Unfortunately, salary surveys never work like that. The compensation firm does its research and comes back with: here's the range of pay for the job and at the moment you're paying just below the median. Ah-ha! How can you stand tall and say you're a top firm if you don't pay in the top quartile? There you go, you've just increased your wage bill by $x\%$.

The problem is, you're on a no-win treadmill. So you finish your survey and move your pay levels up to the top quartile. Then your competitor down the road does his annual survey and finds out whoops, now he's slipped from top quartile to below the median. He must raise his base by x%! And so on ad infinitum.

This is why CEO and board-level pay packages have gone stratospheric over the last decade – with a lot more moolah at stake. Which board compensation committee can look its CEO in the eye and say they're not going to give him or her a package in the top quartile or even in the top decile? Oh and by the way, the data comes from compensation consultants who are hired by the same people whose pay they are evaluating.

VARIABLE PAY

Increasing the variable component of total pay can be a good idea. But don't do it expecting to reduce cost. Do it to increase staff motivation and to reduce business risk and earnings volatility.

The John Lewis retail group in the UK runs two big chains, John Lewis department stores and Waitrose grocery supermarkets. It is unusual in being the UK's largest example of worker co-ownership, a workers' cooperative. All 60,000 employees are partners and share in the profits. So the variable performance-based part of total pay is unusually high: in 2008 each employee received 20% of base pay (over 10 weeks' pay) as profit share bonus. Customer service and staff attitudes are outstanding. Both businesses are gaining market share and have some of the highest profit margins in their sectors.

At the other end of the pay spectrum, partners in consulting or investment banking firms take low base salaries and get most of their compensation from the year-end profit share, which can be 10 or 20 times base pay.

In general, making compensation more variable doesn't cut long-run cost. Most people are unwilling to accept cuts in base pay in exchange for the possibility of a larger variable payment. Any increase in the variable component becomes an add-on to a current base package. Even if the recipient agrees to forgo increases in base for one or two years to fund the extra variable, total cost goes up.

There is also the problem of defining the basis for paying out the variable – the performance targets.

I used to think you could get really scientific about using targets to change and motivate people. An enterprise software sales team in the US beat this delusion out of me. I was CFO and had to construct the sales commission model. Every month I thought I had it nailed and every month the sales director came up with reasons we had to change it. Coincidentally, every change increased the commission due on what had been sold that month. Despite my cunning plans, the model had no observable impact on what the sales teams did on a Monday morning. Worst of all, the commission payments bore no relation at all to whether the business was doing well, or even in the end whether there had been any sales that month. One month we had zero sales but the sales director calculated that he had met all his MBOs (management by objectives), like motivating his team and phoning some customers, so he was still due 40% of maximum bonus payout. We had reached the nadir of paying sales commission on zero sales. (He was of course completely unembarrassed by this paradox.)

The best way to pay large bonuses or commissions is to pay them based on overall business results, not individual micro targets. So it's an unequivocal win–win for the business and for the bonus recipient and there's no argument about how to measure outcomes. The John Lewis and professional partnership payments are in that category.

Unfortunately you won't be able to hire any software salespeople on that basis, so you're going to have to go on wrestling with issues like is a sale still a sale for commission purposes if the customer never pays? Answers on a postcard please to the software sales convention in Las Vegas.

Technology and Productivity

New technology can transform the people cost equation by radically increasing productivity, or by completely automating or eliminating labor processes.

Take grocery shopping. Checkout productivity has been transformed by barcoding, checkout scanners and point-of-sale terminals – a modern checkout clerk can process transactions five or ten times faster than someone on the till in the 1950s. Backroom productivity has been transformed by logistics and supply-chain innovation, including supplier data exchanges, containerization, handheld terminals, RFID (radio-frequency identification, microchips costing one or two cents embedded in products to enable their automated location and tracking). In many cases labor is or could be totally eliminated – like checkout clerks by self-checkouts or stock taking by RFID tracking.

Technology can now reach the softer, more touchy-feely, non-production-line parts of a business. Take personal sales in a business-to-business environment. Historically this activity was very unautomated, very low tech. Individual productivity depended on the personal character of your salesperson. Team productivity depended on informal and unreliable personal interaction. But now even this low-tech stronghold is being invaded. New software offerings like Salesforce.com give you tools to manage and prioritize sales time and to leverage assets better across a whole sales team. Multichannel selling tools allow you to slice and dice sales contact, and so sales cost, between face to face, phone, email, messaging and self-help.

I work with a business-to-business company that had been very traditional in its management of field sales. The average full cost of a field salesperson is over $100,000, but until recently it had made almost no real investment in software, hardware or communications to get the best productivity out of that $100,000. Now it is investing

71

RIDING THE UTILIZATION WAVE: PEAKS AND TROUGHS

People should be utilized most of the time, not sitting around with nothing to do. This principle is well applied in manning conveyor belts and supermarket checkouts. There are sometimes opportunities in less obvious areas.

A Swiss-based business had discrete teams working on credit control, telesales and customer service (phone/email). A peaks-and-troughs analysis for these three functions showed complementary demand patterns: customer service demand was highest in the morning; telesales calls were most effective at the end of the day; and credit control (chasing up payments) was best done before and after lunch. Looking at team skills, while some people would clearly only be effective in one role, several people were easily capable of learning and handling two or even three roles. So we left 50% of the workload to be dealt with by dedicated one-role teams, but we created a shared-role team that would move through the day from customer service to credit control to telesales. We got about a 10% overall productivity gain and an increase in effectiveness in the shared-role team, whose members were now more engaged by their jobs.

Technology was key. Role sharing was possible because team members had desktop access to a "360-degree" customer view, letting them see a unified history of sales, payments and service issues.

Technology can also change and smooth the demand pattern. An intelligent email- and FAQ-based customer service lets you inventory customer problems so they can be dealt with in quieter periods.

about $1,500–2,000 a year extra per salesperson in a bundle of productivity tools. That 2% increase in cost should get it at least a 10% increase in sales output.

Investments in new technology should only be made after all possible productivity gains have been achieved without new technology – by simply working on activity logic, activity flow and workforce behavior. This is a basic premise of good IT projects: don't automate bad practice.

Line managers need to be regularly prompted to do zero-based thinking about why and how they do things and whether any new approaches exist. Chief information officers and IT managers should champion the search for new technologies that could drive productivity and be asked to present their ideas to the executive team and the board every year.

Firing

Here's the nub of managing people cost. Why do managers find it so difficult to confront firing decisions, even in clear situations of underperformance, failure or mismatch with the job? Is it because they are deeply caring individuals who can't bring themselves to be unkind?

Well maybe, sometimes. But I'm pretty skeptical. More often it's because they don't want to be seen as the bad guy. Or have unpleasant one-on-one termination conversations. Or because their peers, and the well-performing staff, are telling them that any firings will devastate morale, all the good people will leave too and the organization will collapse. None of which is true.

Getting rid of underperformers lets an organization breathe. It removes a burden of cost and wasted time. It raises morale. A few weeks after you do it, the people who were saying it would destroy team spirit are asking why you didn't do it sooner. You get savings over and above the direct cost of terminated staff as well. Unproductive employees arrange meetings and projects that suck up the time of productive staff to no purpose. They need lots of reviews and stroking from their bosses.

I had a head of business development once who epitomized this. After he was fired it emerged that he had been the prime mover behind a raft of fluffy projects and initiatives. Nobody else thought these were of any practical value, but they had been consuming a day a week of middle manager time in rambling brainstorming sessions. With him gone, these middle managers suddenly had 20% more time for useful work.

Cutting out dead wood boosts organizational morale. Good performers see that merit is recognized and rewarded and bad performance is penalized. They get to work with a peer group they respect. They feel part of an efficient organization with high standards.

They may tell you the opposite before any firing program, because it's human nature to sympathize with people who are losing their jobs. In the run-up to terminations the halls buzz with shock-horror rumor and speculation. The business is collapsing. The managers are short-term swine. If *she* goes then *we* are all leaving and *they* are stuffed.

My first experience of this was at BCG (Boston Consulting Group) in Boston in 1983. I was summer interning between my two Harvard MBA years. BCG was still the sexiest company to work for, the pioneer of strategy consulting with its cow/dog/star matrices and scale/learning curves. It had been in stellar growth mode for over a decade.

I was there when it decided to have its first ever staff shakeout. I think it ended up firing about a third of its senior managers and junior partners. For a growth company this was (and always is) a traumatic moment, a horrible baptism in business reality. The corridors and coffee machines were slippery with blood, with predictions of total business implosion, of an irreversible evisceration of the BCG culture. The golden days were over.

In fact the business blossomed and bloomed and the shoots of growth pushed with new vigor, as they continued to do over the next two decades with regular bursts of dead-wood pruning.

There are two main approaches to getting rid of dead wood.

You could say I'll do it as and when it's necessary. So one year 15% of heads get chopped, the next year zero. The level of chopping could be down to staff performance or to business results. This is OK, but it doesn't force managers to make tough people decisions regularly.

The alternative is forced ranking. Every year each manager has to rank staff from top to bottom, by name, and the bottom x% have to go. You could structure this ranking by function, by job level, by business unit. Jack Welch used this approach at GE.

Forced ranking is controversial. It is used a lot in America but little in Europe. Critics see it as heartless, denying any long-term duty of care and nurture, dumping people the moment they lose utility, denying the possibility of personal improvement. European companies are uncomfortable with such a tooth-and-claw approach to staff. They also, on the flip side, don't like to reward outstanding performers as extravagantly as US companies do.

A Spanish CEO I know well says that I am an Anglo-Saxon cost cutter deep in my bones. He is right on many fronts, but on this issue actually I take a mid-Atlantic position. I like a rolling two-year forced ranking, combining tough performance management with a reasonable commitment to try to recover bad performers. Every year you do the ranking and if someone stays in the bottom 5% or 10% for two years running then they're out. That gives you (and them) a year to try to turn them around, with the spotlight full on.

Absent of this discipline management tends to go mushy. I respect my Spanish CEO friend, but he is soft on getting rid of bad performers. At his technology center there was not one single involuntary termination (out of 2,000 staff) in five years. The staff there were pretty committed and hard working, but they knew that at the end of the day there would be no repercussions if they didn't deliver. So key projects slipped and market opportunities were lost.

If you practice tough people management you have to be seen to be fair and consistent in how you arrive at tough decisions. A good appraisal and review process, one that you stick to rigorously, is vital.

Consultancies are usually good at this. I have worked with four major consultancies – Booz Allen, BCG, OC&C and PricewaterhouseCoopers (PwC) – and in all cases the staff review process was taken seriously and really followed through. Professional staff were reviewed every six months. The reviewer, a partner or principal, would talk to superiors, peers and subordinates. The review would be approved by a partner committee then given one on one to the staff member. Conclusions and actions were documented and explicit. Is the person on track, for what, when? If not on track, what needs to be fixed, in what timeframe, otherwise when could there be a parting of the ways? If at the end of this process the outcome was negative and someone was counselled out, then at least the process and conclusions were open, fact based and fair.

In contrast, I could come up with a long list of organizations that are poor at this. They talk about being people-and-talent businesses and on paper they have detailed appraisal and review processes, policed by large HR departments. But in practice appraisals and feedbacks only get done if they are good news. Nothing that really matters, like promotions, salary increases or terminations, is tied to the process – those key decisions are made on separate tracks. Everybody ducks the confrontation of underperformance.

FIRING BEFORE CHRISTMAS

It's early December, you've just analyzed the cost base and you need to get headcount down by 15%. Do you fire now or wait until after Christmas?

The answer is, fire now.

The obvious reason for firing before Christmas is, well, obvious. If you're going to get cost out, get it out as soon as possible. No point hanging around. Every month you prevaricate and delay is money out of the window for ever.

But there is another reason. It's actually fairer and nicer to staff to fire them before Christmas. The main reason managers don't do it is not because they're really all that caring. It's because they don't want to come across as hard-hearted bastards. But that serves their interest, not the staff getting fired.

I was working with a West Coast company where we had this situation. Everybody knew the business was in trouble and terminations were on the cards. We had the analysis and we knew the names to go. But the CEO didn't want to be a bad guy before Christmas.

All the staff worked 12-hour days throughout the festive period. They didn't cut back on their Christmas spending. When the terminations came in January they were overspent and they'd missed the chance at least to have a relaxing time with the family before they went job hunting.

Fire before Christmas. Grit your teeth and be Scrooge for the season.

TRICKY BEASTS AND TASKFORCES

In any organization there are always people who, if there were any justice, would be the first to go in any cost-cutting program. Everybody knows who they are. *They* know who they are. But there they are, year after year, still getting their paychecks, being promoted even through downsizings and profit improvement programs and radical restructurings. We need to recognize these beasts and their tricky survival strategies.

The classic example in the consulting world is the admin partner. He or she starts off with the accurate title of office manager and does all the boring stuff around running the office: HR, accounting, payroll, buildings and so on. Then at some point the other real partners, who sell big fat projects to big fat clients, are nagged and pestered into turning this into a profit-sharing partner position. From that point on the admin partner is the single biggest and least justifiable overhead cost in the business.

When I was working at Booz Allen in the US I did an internal project looking at how to cut Booz's office overhead costs. We took the Chicago office as a trial analysis. We looked at buildings, travel, IT, graphics and so on. We investigated all the numbers and costs of all the back-office staff: accounting, secretaries, personnel etc. One number stood out: we had an admin partner, call him Bill, over-seeing the whole overhead. Bill was on about $600,000 a year including his profit share. (This was many years ago.) That's an expensive office manager.

We got asked to present our initial ideas to the assembled Chicago back-office team. Not to beat about the bush, we put up a current org chart with all the titles and actual names. Then we put up a proposed new org chart with half the current names missing – in particular, no more admin partner. There was mayhem in the meeting room. Shock-horror outrage. People out on window ledges threat-ening to jump.

Silence from Bill at the back. Then he raised his hand for quiet. "What Andrew's saying is only what's right for the business," he said. "It's what we get asked to do for our clients. We have to do it to ourselves too. I guarantee we can make these savings. And I'm vol-unteering right now to lead the taskforce that's going to achieve them."

This was breathtaking and had to be admired. Of course, three years later Bill was the only member of that group still there, contin-uing to draw his $600,000 a year. So watch out for the guys who vol-unteer to lead the cost-reduction taskforce.

EVENING THE ODDS

Let's switch sides for a moment. Maybe you aren't a hard-driving CEO with a $20 million package, a slash-and-burn paradigm of productivity. Maybe instead you're a harried and harassed middle manager on a modest salary and 2% bonus, 10 years to go to pension, looking for the quiet life.

Uh-oh. Bad luck. Psycho Boss just announced a strategic review of organization and costs. The axe-wielding consultants are coming in. Workshops and offsites are being scheduled. The phrase "dead wood" is in the air.

Just to even the odds, here's how to survive the corporate purges. When the consultants come to interview you, don't say:

"I haven't got time for this. We did all this last year. We can't get any more cost out. You consultants don't understand the business. Everyone's demoralized. It's stupid, we're cutting into muscle now, there's no fat. No, I haven't got any cost data, you'll have to ask finance. We're only doing this so Psycho Boss can strut around being macho with the press. What about his pay packet, that costs more than my whole department? I can't give you time for another meeting for about two months. Actually I'm quite tired today. You know, I've always hated consultants."

No, no, no. You're signing up to the Dead Wood Society. Say this:

"What a great opportunity. I've been saying for months we're organizationally overweight. That's a great list of questions – I'll get my team to give you the data tomorrow. What I like about Psycho Boss is he grips the bull by the horns, no bullshit. I hope I can lead the next brainstorm? It must be fascinating being a consultant, all those insights, all that MBA brainpower. When's our next meeting? Let's get busy!"

Remember, Beria survived 20 years of Stalin and lived to put the old bastard in his coffin.

Managing the Average Performer

In the half-light between obvious stars and obvious firings sit the majority of employees, the average performers. Problems of people cost management can center on the challenge of these people. After all, even very protective organizations eventually get rid of total dead wood and stars don't need to justify their costs.

Average performers are frustrating because they're not as good, not as productive, as we'd like them to be. But they're not bad and they can work very long hours with a lot of commitment, so it's hard to give them a tough appraisal. There's no obvious trigger for change – no basis for a big wake-up-and-shake-up appraisal or a radical up or down move, a promotion or firing. This can be OK when the employee is fresh in the job or the organization is young. But as time passes inertia sets in, commitment erodes and productivity starts to really decline. Employer and employee get more frustrated and unhappy. Are there any solutions?

I have worked in an industry whose core competence is managing top-end professional talent, strategy consulting. In a similar way to the forced ranking we've already discussed, my industry tackles the average performer problem very directly: via up-or-out career paths. At any career stage up to partner you're either on your way up the career ladder or you're being counselled out. Each step on the ladder lasts between two and four years. So let's say you've just been hired into Bain or OC&C as a consultant out of business school. The baseline career path is that you have three years to make manager, then three years to make principal, then three years to make junior partner. If you're 26 coming out of business school you should be looking at junior partner by 35. You might slip or accelerate by plus or minus a year at any stage, but you have to be broadly on that track. If you come of it you start to be counselled out. Only when you reach senior partner are you safe from the up-or-out culture.

The core discipline in such an approach is regular formal appraisals. Strategy consulting firms spend a very large amount of time on the appraisal process. And that time is partner time, not junior staff or the HR department. Appraisals are at least annual and often six-monthly. They are 360-degree appraisals, with input from managers, peers and subordinates. They are reviewed and signed off by several partners before being given to the employee. There is a full record trail that can be gone back into at any point.

Obviously a total up-or-out culture won't work in many larger organizations with a broader base of job types and talents. But most organizations could and should operate much closer to that consulting model than they do.

First, they should institutionalize a strong appraisal process. This is the *sine qua non* of people management. A strong process has to have the elements described in consulting: rigor, consistent follow-through, leadership and involvement from senior line managers, 360-degree input, full documentation and a record trail.

I should mention here a useful trick to force appraisers to be honest and tough. Each appraiser has to say whether, given the option, he or she would use the appraisee again on another project or in another job, and at what level or in what role – the same as before, higher or lower. The appraiser has to stick by that judgment in future staffing decisions, so if you give someone a big tick you can't turn round in six months and refuse to have them on your team.

Secondly, even if organizations cannot implement a real up-or-out dynamic, they should set up a proxy. This can be as simple as forcing the appraisal to judge whether an individual is on an upward, static or downward track and communicating that to the employee. That judgment can then lead to concrete recommendations and actions, for the individual or the organization.

Minimizing the Core Organization

Given the difficulty of managing people cost, a central strategic principle is to keep the core organization of full-time staff down to an absolute minimum.

SUBCONTRACTING

For example, you could contract out most of the components of a product or service and only keep in-house the higher value-added activities, like design, final assembly, brand management.

The top global automakers have been moving along this path for decades, pushing out much of the risk and pain of ups and downs in demand. They subcontract either to specialized component makers who end up being huge global players themselves, like Bosch or Valio; or to fragmented but highly efficient local small businesses, like the network of plastics moldings suppliers in Japan, delivering at 50% of the cost of Toyota or Nissan.

Or take media companies. Back in the 1970s these businesses were very vertically integrated and had strong labor unions. Over the last four decades they have been hollowed out. Production companies, editing houses, cameramen, distribution arms – these have been separated out from the core commissioning and brand-owning business, either to smaller outside companies or to individual contractors. In the process the industry has been deunionized. Rates for most jobs have fallen as labor markets have become more open and competitive.

The hollowing out or unbundling of an enterprise is not just about managing people cost. A narrow focus on a few core businesses and a few core competencies is likely to maximize corporate value. Vertical integration and conglomerate strategies are old hat, looking back to the early days of US Steel and Ford Motor Co., not relevant in today's specialized and efficient markets.

OUTSOURCING

You can also minimize the core organization by outsourcing whole administrative functions, like IT, personnel records, payroll, financial processing. Huge businesses have been built around this trend, including hundreds of thousands of people employed by Accenture, IBM Global Services, EDS and PwC, in the West and in offshore locations like India and the Philippines.

As with component suppliers, there can be reasons other than people cost for outsourcing. In IT, for example, a large specialist can get scale advantage in the cost of data centers or networks or hardware purchasing, and can stay up to speed more easily on technology developments. Nevertheless, a prime motivation for most outsourcing moves is to shift the burden of people cost management outside, onto the outsourcer.

An outsourcer of insurance claims processing has no material cost other than people, so is going to be obsessed with keeping that cost as low and flexible as possible. Its client, the outsourcing insurer, wants to focus on the high value added of product development, actuarial skills, branding and distribution. If claims processing stayed in the core organization the claims-processing staff would probably end up overpaid and underproductive. And if there is a business downturn the trauma of downsizing is transferred to the outsourcer.

Pushing activities out to subcontractors and outsourcers does not mean the costs no longer need to get managed, however. In-house people cost goes away, but the cost becomes a supplier cost and managing suppliers brings a different set of challenges, which we'll look at in the next chapter.

Toolkit – People

THE BASICS

○ Recognize that people costs are sticky, go up relentlessly and are always larger than you think.

○ Get a strong cost-oriented HR function to play the lead in managing people cost.

HIRING

○ Capitalize hiring decisions and treat them like capital investments.

○ Minimize risk, maximize flexibility.

PAYING

○ Hold your nerve, stay firm.

○ Watch out for the salary survey cost escalator.

○ Don't look to variable compensation programs for cost reduction.

TECHNOLOGY AND PRODUCTIVITY

○ Continually look for ways to transform productivity…

○ …first without new technology – don't automate bad practice.

○ …second with new technology – including ways of eliminating an activity completely.

○ Require line managers to do zero-based reviews of activities.

○ Get CIOs and IT heads to trawl for new ideas.

FIRING

○ Clear out dead wood, the organization will thank you.

○ Do it proactively, earlier rather than later.

○ Prune with a rolling two-year forced ranking.

○ Stick to a rigorous appraisal and review process.

○ Watch out for taskforce volunteers.

MINIMIZE THE CORE ORGANIZATION

○ Push component supply and low-value functions out to subcontractors and outsourcers.

○ Replace empire building with a minimize-core mindset.

5

Suppliers

Distant cousins, there's a limited supply…
Big Eyed Beans from Venus! Oh my, oh my.

In the last chapter I looked at the costs of people, of in-house staff. These costs are difficult to manage, with a lot of emotion, inertia, ducking and diving around tough decisions. To manage people cost you need to be tough and tenacious.

Now I'm turning to all other types of cost. I've lumped them together and called them "supplier" costs. These are costs that people like to manage and enjoy getting tough with. It's fun to bang the table in a supplier meeting, demanding price cuts and better service, threatening to take your business elsewhere. It's a lot more fun than counselling out an underperforming member of staff.

But just because it's more fun doesn't mean it gets done very well. A table-banging approach to supplier management will only get you so far. To manage supplier cost, you need to be smart and structured.

Who Manages Supplier Costs?

There are three main players in external supplier cost management.

There's the buyer, in a retail or wholesale business. This can be a very nice job. A fashion buyer gets to review new ranges, study fashion magazines, visit suppliers in exotic locations, stroll down the King's Road absorbing the new season's vibe. A packaged grocery buyer with Tesco or Wal-Mart gets the top sales and marketing teams from P&G filing through his or her office begging for shelf space and end-of-aisle displays.

A young Frenchwoman I know is the seafood buyer for Brake Brothers, a top European wholesaler to caterers. She spends her time visiting fishermen and fish processors in Japan and Nova Scotia, oyster and shrimp farms in Arcachon and Northern Spain, cod trawlers off Iceland. She is a world expert on the ecology, biology and economics of fishing.

Top buyers come very high up in the management food chain. The head of buying (or of buying and merchandising, or of trading) is usually the most senior executive under the CEO and sits on the board. Most retail or wholesale CEOs have come up through the buying ranks.

Then there's the manager of purchasing or sourcing in a manufacturing business. This is a muscular kind of job. You get to mess around with auto components, steel, unprocessed foods, oils and plastics. You get to arm-wrestle with grizzled sales reps and traders, navigate global supply chains, track spot prices. You feed in to complex production schedules, making sure the line doesn't go down but keeping prices and inventory tight. The head of production insists on your head on a platter if you get it wrong. To burn off stress you work out with weights, building up your abs and pecs.

Purchasing or sourcing managers are pretty high up the food chain, although not as high as buyers. They usually report to a head of production (or manufacturing) and it's the head of production who sits at the top table.

Lastly, there's the procurement manager, who could also be the purchasing manager in a services business. This is the function that looks after "all other" costs – those that are left after you've taken out people and products from a retail business, or people and production lines from a manufacturing business. These "all other" external supplier costs include:

○ Non-manufacturing equipment, IT hardware and software
○ Non-manufacturing property and facilities, including stores and branches
○ Office supplies
○ Communications
○ Travel
○ Catering, cleaning, other operational services
○ Outsourced back-office activities (accounting, processing, HR)
○ Sales and marketing services (exhibitions, media buying, PR)
○ Financial services (insurance, banking, accounting, payroll)
○ Other professional services (consulting, legal)

Ten years ago many businesses would not have had a procurement manager. These costs would have been managed at lower levels in the organization, by office managers or support staff; or sometimes not at all, in the cases of travel, communications and professional services.

In the late 1980s I did a project on institutional catering in the UK. The biggest British buyer of catering services was the National Health Service, spending billions of dollars. There was one central NHS procurement manager looking after this huge spend. I went to interview him in his office in Hannibal House, a famously awful office block in the middle of a famously awful pink shopping center called the Elephant and Castle in South London. The elevator up to his floor smelt like a tenement block. The reception area looked like a British Rail waiting room. His secretary came out to collect me, wearing fluffy slippers and a flower-patterned plastic overall, fag on lip. She shuffled me down a gray corridor. Mr. Procurement Manager was wearing corduroy trousers and a jacket with worn elbow patches. He was very excited because he had just discovered a whole new catering concept called McDonald's. What did I think of it, could he put it in every NHS hospital?

Things have changed. Now the professional procurement manager has arrived, armed with an MBA and ISO 9000 certification, to get a grip on these slippery and unglamorous cost areas. And procurement now has status and clout, reporting in to the CFO or COO.

There are also some big chunks of activity and cost where external supplier costs are managed by central functional heads, mainly of supply chain (or distribution or logistics), marketing, property and IT. Even if an organization has a procurement manager, these areas of cost may be outside his or her remit and left to the functional head.

Understand the Balance of Power

Understanding and playing the balance of power between buyer and supplier is a key skill in supplier management.

You need to understand how important your business is to the supplier – what percentage of its revenue or profits you represent. And how important the supplier is to you – what percentage of your costs it represents, how critical it is to the functioning of your business, how easily you could find a substitute. This will give a matrix of situations like the one opposite.

The bottom right box is no problem. Neither matters very much to the other. You can manage these suppliers in a tactical way, making sure you're efficient at getting the best prices, regularly casting the net for new vendors.

The bottom left box is also no problem. You have the power. The challenge here is to stop short of driving good suppliers into the ground.

The top right box is a problem. You are very vulnerable to price hikes. You need to find substitutes and cut switching cost, to reduce dependence on the supplier.

The top left box is a complex, mutually interdependent relationship: a strong buyer and a strong supplier. Examples would be:

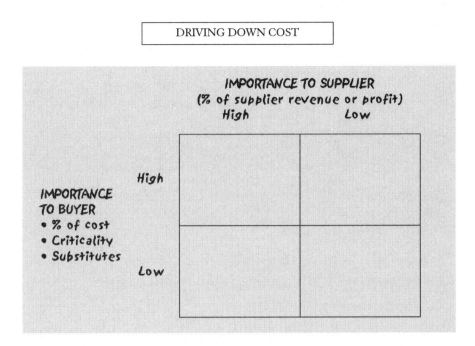

○ Wal-Mart or Tesco dealing with P&G or Diageo, or Dell dealing with Intel.

○ The UK government dealing with EDS on a five-year contract to computerize the National Health Service.

○ Dealing with a builder when he's halfway through building a conservatory extension, he's running late and over budget, you have no heating and no kitchen and winter is drawing in (yes, that could be a personal example).

In this top left box you have to find sensible win–win strategies. Both sides will test and push the balance of power, trying to get a bigger piece of the profit pie. You need to be tough but smart, focusing on the joint opportunity, the total pie.

We can summarize issues and strategies on the matrix overleaf.

Consolidate to Fewer Better Suppliers

Most businesses can gain by consolidating their supplier base. Higher volume per supplier usually gets you better prices. This

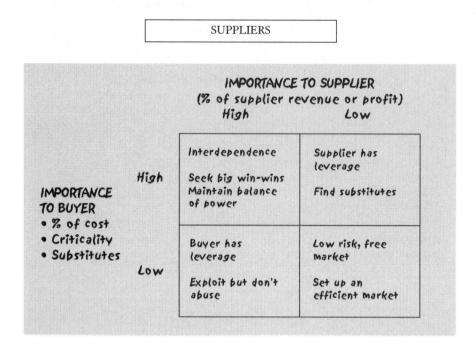

could be from sheer buying clout or it could be from supplier economies of scale – longer production runs, spreading of fixed cost.

Having fewer suppliers also gives you more account planning time with each one, to figure out ways of working better together to mutual advantage and to apply best practices to the total supply chain.

In the early 1990s I was working on the restructuring of a weak UK grocery retail chain, then called Gateway and now called Somerfield. We were doing competitive analysis, looking at Gateway's buying and selling prices compared with other UK grocers. We were confused as to how Kwiksave, a much smaller chain, seemed to be getting the same or better prices from suppliers in category after category. Then we realized it was a function of concentration. For an individual product category (say baked beans) the numbers might have looked like those opposite.

Gateway had twice Kwiksave's overall sales volume, but it had 2.5 times the number of suppliers so volume per supplier was less than Kwiksave. On top of that Kwiksave had a much narrower range of stock-keeping units, so its volume per SKU was 2.5 times that of Gateway. Net result: Kwiksave could get a 2% buying cost advantage

Category economics, illustrative

	Gateway	Kwiksave	Gateway/ Kwiksave
Overall sales volume, index	100	50	2.0
Suppliers	10	4	
Volume per supplier	10	12.5	0.8
SKUs (stock-keeping units)	50	10	
Volume per SKU	2	5	0.4
Unit buying price (index)	100	98	

over Gateway despite its much smaller overall size. One of our first restructuring tasks was to reduce Gateway's suppliers by at least a third and reduce the number of SKUs per supplier.

Microsoft buys in a huge volume of contract development and IT services, in the US and offshore. For many years supplier selection was decentralized, down to small departments and groups of developers. The result was hundreds of different suppliers, most subscale and inefficient, and a wild variation in quality. Then the corporate center got a grip on the supply base, consolidating down to half a dozen or so primary approved vendors in each service category. Result: more consistent delivery and lower prices, and more effective sharing of best practice between Microsoft departments and between Microsoft and approved vendors.

This kind of consolidation process should not produce a supplier shortlist that is frozen for all time. Every year the core list should be reviewed, the worst 5–10% of suppliers culled and promising new blood added.

The only type of supplier situation where regular weeding out and consolidation aren't important is the bottom right box on the matrix opposite, where you aren't important to the suppliers and they aren't important to you. You can run these situations as an open marketplace with a long list of potential vendors. (You can still demand that all suppliers get approved vendor screening before they're allowed on the list, though.)

Negotiate Intelligently

Optimizing your relationship with your suppliers isn't just about who has the power, who can do the kicking. Even when you hold the cards, you need to invest time in relationships with key suppliers and be an intelligent negotiator.

UNDERSTAND YOUR SUPPLIERS'
ECONOMICS AND TRY TO FIND WIN-WINS

Don't just focus on the price being charged, understand how the total supply chain fits together. Spend time with key suppliers to build this understanding in regular review meetings that aren't just about price negotiation.

Take the interplay between consumer goods retailers and manufacturers. In the past, the two ends of the grocery supply chain kept their inventory and order systems separate and opaque from each other. This created multiple buffer stocks, errors in delivery and reordering, multiple checking and handling costs, high product wastage and returns. Over the last decade retailers like Wal-Mart have worked with producers like P&G to exchange data and coordinate the supply chain. The result has been a big reduction in overall costs, inventory, shipping errors and out-of-stocks.

DON'T NEGOTIATE SO HARD THAT
THERE'S NO PROFIT IN IT FOR THE SUPPLIER

This may be enjoyably macho, for one pricing round. But it is unsustainable and self-defeating – churning suppliers can be more costly in the long run. Understanding the economics will help you know what a supplier's real bottom line is. And you can still play hardball: an important customer can define the bottom line as after just marginal cost.

In the UK, Marks & Spencer was for many years a successful example of symbiosis between a very strong retail buyer and a few preferred key suppliers. Dewhirst was one of its key UK-based clothing suppliers. Over a 10-year cycle ending in the mid-1990s both businesses earned a 20–25% return on capital, although Dewhirst's returns were volatile, while M&S's were as consistent as GE's under Jack Welch. M&S was happy to let key suppliers make good money as long as they absorbed more of the pain of the economic cycle.

(M&S's performance collapsed recently, but that was nothing to do with its old strategy of close partnership with key suppliers, which was very successful for decades. And it now seems to be on a good recovery path.)

CONSOLIDATE YOUR BUYING POWER – ENCOURAGE
SUPPLIERS TO SET UP GLOBAL KEY ACCOUNT MANAGEMENT

In large multinational businesses buying is usually still decentralized, across different departments, territories and business units. Local managers resist centralization because they think it will slow things down, force them to use suppliers they don't like, or stick them with centrally negotiated prices that are worse than what they can get locally. The local managers have a strong point – you don't want more bureaucracy.

And in fact you can get most of the benefit without actually centralizing. Say you are a central manager in a global hotel chain, like Accor or Marriott. One of your major purchases is commercial cleaning and sanitation services. Buying decisions are made at country or individual property level. Hotels use some local suppliers, but most also use big global suppliers like Ecolab. You want to get the full benefit of your overall buying power with Ecolab without messing up local flexibility and accountability.

You need two bits of data: your total global spend with Ecolab and differences in pricing across countries (there always are differences). Armed with that, you can threaten to veto Ecolab as a supplier unless it cuts you a better deal globally. And you can demand that pricing gravitate toward the cheapest country level (allowing for any real differences in local cost to serve). You can do all this without changing the fact that all buying decisions at the end of the day get made locally; which is fine for you, as a tough local buyer may drive down his local price and so give you a lower benchmark for global negotiations.

Encourage your suppliers to give you a key account manager to deal with you in the center and negotiate across all territories and business units. Once a key account manager is in place, your business is their whole life and they will walk through fire to get you the best deal possible – their end-of-year bonus will be based on global sales to you, and heaven help them if they actually lose you as a key account.

FIGURE OUT THE BEST TRADEOFF
BETWEEN PRICE AND PAYMENT TERMS

Don't squeeze suppliers on both price and payment terms. Whoever has the lowest cost of capital should take on the greater cash-flow burden in exchange for better pricing. For example, large, well-capitalized fashion retailers in the West buy from small-scale, under-capitalized clothing producers in China. The retail chains have lower cost of capital and stronger cash positions. They should be able to offer faster payment in return for deeper price cuts and still come out better off.

CONSIDER BOTH BUNDLING AND UNBUNDLING

When you look at the supplier's value chain, consider if you could get more value either by more bundling of activities or by unbundling. Bundling could reduce hand-off and interdependency costs, while unbundling could allow you to leverage more efficient specialists.

Don't Get Locked In

If you can't walk away from a supplier, sooner or later you'll end up paying over the odds. To avoid getting locked in:

○ Always have at least one other supplier as a credible alternative. It may be better to spread your business over two suppliers, even if you pay a bit more.
○ Work on reducing the cost of switching – time, money, risk, technical difficulty.
○ Avoid long-term contracts unless there are overwhelming economic advantages.
○ Maintain an active marketplace.

As an example, take GDSs: global distribution systems, the computer networks through which travel agents make airline bookings, with airlines paying the GDSs a fee per booking. Each of the two main ones, Sabre and Amadeus, has about 30% global market share.

GDSs were set up in the 1970s and 1980s. Until the internet arrived they had a great lock-in business. It was hard to win a travel agency contract, but once you were in it was very hard to get kicked out. Each GDS installed its own proprietary terminals inside an agency with private network connectivity. Agencies almost never installed two systems side by side. Agents were trained up on how to use a system's cryptic formats and each system had lots of idiosyncrasies, so it would take months for an agent to get productive on a new GDS. Agencies signed four- or five-year contracts with financial penalties for pulling out early.

Net result: when I started working on the business in the US in 1997, only 2% of travel agencies switched their GDS supplier in any one year. GDSs, along with privatized airports, were one of the few really profitable pieces of the air travel industry, able to raise prices year on year faster than inflation.

But then the internet sprung the lock. Agents could now switch between different GDSs booking by booking, on a standard PC on a normal open broadband connection. Booking screens changed from cryptic green ones, which took time to learn, to intuitive graphics, cutting training time. Agencies now sign GDS contracts, if at all, on an annual renewal basis. They can also book on airlines' own websites rather than via the GDS; in fact they have to if they want to book with a low-cost airline.

So the old GDS lock-in is declining. It is still a profitable business, but prices are under intense pressure and making great returns has got much harder.

You can also get trapped in horrible lock-ins with property cost. In a booming market you are sucked into paying top-end rates and taking on five-year, no-get-out leases. When the demand bubble pops you get hit twice: you're paying double the real market rate per square foot, and you can't unload the space you no longer need (now you've downsized) at any price for several years. In a frothy market it's better to trade off a higher rate for a shorter lease, or to squeeze more capacity out of existing space for one or two years.

The public sector, never the sharpest at negotiation, tends to get locked in to very long-term outsourcing contracts. For example, since the mid-1990s the UK government has been awarding PFI (Private Finance Initiative) contracts to private companies to invest in and run hospitals, schools, prisons, transport systems and the like. The government gets the double benefit of cost savings from outsourcing (a reasonable argument) and off-balance-sheet financing of public-sector capital expenditure (a bit of a scam to make government finances look better).

Recently a famous television chef, Jamie Oliver, exposed the scandalously low standard of food being served to children in British schools. Average budget per meal per child was equivalent to about one dollar. The meals were deep-fried fat, sugar and salt, with 10% reconstituted meat scrapings. Politicians fell over each other leaping onto a reform-school-meals bandwagon and the government pledged an immediate revolution. Then it emerged that hundreds of schools were locked into 25-year PFI contracts with outside catering suppliers, and these had severe financial penalties for any contract changes. The PFI contractors had built reconstituted Turkey Twizzlers into their contractual business cases, as well as the profits from thousands of vending machines selling fizzy, fatty, salty junk. A 25-year contract might be OK for the Channel Tunnel, but it is pure insanity for a simple low-investment catering operation.

As well as contractual or operational lock-ins, there are lock-ins based on pure habit and inertia.

Banks rely heavily on customer inertia. Once they've opened an account most people can't be bothered to switch accounts, or even to check whether they're still getting good rates. So banks suck in new business at loss-leader prices, then quietly do a rate switch after six months. And many people simply forget they've got money in old savings and checking accounts. I once worked with a small local S&L (Savings & Loan) in New York where 20% of deposits were dormant and earning zero interest.

SHOULD YOU *ALWAYS* MAINTAIN AT LEAST TWO POTENTIAL SUPPLIERS?

Yes in maybe 95% or 99% of cases. But there may be some unusual situations in which alternative strategies are better.

I was recently working with a business that was the main European buyer of an unusual piece of capital equipment. There were only two competing manufacturers, the overall market for this type of equipment was small, neither manufacturer was making any material money out of the business, neither had invested anything in product development for years, and both were always teetering on the edge of bankruptcy.

My client wanted to reduce purchase cost but also wanted to see some investment being made in a new-generation product range.

In this case the right conclusion was to consolidate volume with one supplier, even though the likely result was that the other supplier would go bust, so in future we would have no competitive supply alternative. With extra volume, the one remaining supplier could drive down unit cost and price but finally achieve reasonable profit margins and so become interested in and capable of making investment in new product development.

We recognized the long-term risk of becoming hostage to one supplier. But in this case we still held enough negotiating ammunition: in any year we could choose to defer new purchases and survive for quite a while by renovating and recycling old equipment. One year's purchase deferral by my client would be enough to wipe out the supplier's profits for that year – a threat that was as effective as having a competitor.

So it is very important to maintain an active marketplace with your suppliers, to avoid inertia and creeping inefficiency:

○ Make sure that big supply contracts go through a regular retendering process.
○ Review approved supplier lists at least once a year.
○ Consider setting up B2B ecommerce marketplaces for smaller purchase categories with many vendors, for regular purchasing of commodities, or for buying and selling clearance goods.

Manage Total Cost of Ownership

Managing total cost of ownership (TCO) is a valuable tool for thinking through capex decisions. With a TCO approach you don't just focus on obvious upfront costs. You look at ongoing costs in future years, like maintenance and repairs. And you factor in the non-obvious costs, like the time of your own employees.

A modest personal example would be buying a home printer. Printers are pretty much given away these days. The key TCO costs are ink cartridges, which are very expensive, and whether the machine will break down. So my TCO equation = purchase price + lifetime spend on cartridges + risk of breaking down. Cartridge spend is the biggest piece and depends on whether there are cheap compatibles available, which there might be for HP but not for Dell.

Let's take a bigger and more radical example: CRM (customer relationship management) software. CRM software automates and enhances customer interaction for sales, marketing and service, including maintaining customer profiles and history.

CRM used to be sold in the classic enterprise software way: it was very expensive, you were locked in for years at high ongoing cost, you had big indirect costs to get it up and running, and you were taking on a huge risk. The big elephant player in CRM in the late 1990s was Siebel, set up by Tom Siebel who was previously Oracle's top sales guy, so he knew the enterprise sales process.

A typical Siebel big corporate sale would quote a $10m upfront license cost – this was the headline number, the one that the Siebel sales team would try to get put forward as the capex decision. But the real TCO was three or four times that number:

○ An ongoing 15% maintenance charge, that's $1.5m a year, making over $10m present value cost.
○ External deployment costs ("professional services") of $5–10m, paid to Siebel or to somebody like Accenture.
○ Internal staff time spent in the deployment process, with a real cost at least equivalent to the Siebel deployment charges, so at least another $5–10m.

This didn't even factor in the risk cost. You couldn't do a low-cost trial for $100,000, you had to make a huge bet and buy the whole package. And then you had the risk of being locked into this big software edifice; changing your mind later, or trying to flex what you had, would be difficult and expensive.

Siebel's own economic model to sell this monster of a proposition was very high cost: big beast enterprise sales guys on million-dollar commissions, large in-person sales teams on every sales call, no-expense-spared marketing programs. In its peak growth year Siebel was one of the top recruiters at Harvard Business School, beating out McKinsey and Goldman Sachs, just to hire an MBA machine churning out sexy PowerPoints for sales presentations.

Then along came Salesforce.com. This is one of the most successful, maybe *the* most successful, new corporate software businesses of the last decade. It changed the whole economics of CRM.

With Salesforce, you can buy a license for one salesperson. In 2008 the basic cost would be around $65 per person ("per seat") per month; you could buy a small team license, for up to five people, for

$1,200 a year. So you can trial it in a small way (free for 30 days), find out if it works and get the organization slowly on board and getting value out of it, without a big bucks or big bang process. The application is an on-demand hosted service, so you don't need to go through a major IT deployment and corporate integration cycle. It's flexible: you can increase or reduce seats as and when you want.

Salesforce knew that most customers of the old CRM systems hated them, so it made a big deal about breaking with every element of the old approach under a great banner slogan: "No software!" (Not true, but a good grab.) It dramatically changed the TCO for CRM. No huge upfront license fee, no ongoing maintenance cost, no large deployment process, much less risk around trialing and future flexibility.

In mid-2007 Salesforce.com formed a global alliance with Google. The disrupter of personal computing was getting together with the disrupter of corporate computing.

Get Tough on the Costs of Services

A bright management spotlight gets shone on bought-in products (for a retailer) or production supplies (for a manufacturer). In contrast, managing the costs of services is usually a mushroom-like activity, obscure and hidden. But services costs (or SG&A costs: sales, general and administrative) are often the cost lines that are growing fastest: labor-intensive sales, service and admin functions, professional services, IT, outsourcing, property.

Getting tough on SG&A can deliver big savings.

CENTRAL PROCUREMENT

A central procurement function can make sure that good buying practices are introduced and applied across all SG&A cost buckets:

understanding supplier economics, fewer and better suppliers, intelligent negotiation, avoiding lock-in.

This central function doesn't need to be top heavy, it can be one or two people. And it doesn't need actually to make the buying decisions, those can still be made by line managers. It must not become a layer of bureaucracy and documentation, adding no real value, so keep it very slim.

I like to put this function under the CFO. It is a good fit and puts procurement at the right reporting level. You could put it with purchasing or buying as a second-best option. Reporting directly to the CEO is too elevated.

Let's look at some specific cost challenges within SG&A, challenges that procurement can help address.

PROFESSIONAL SERVICES

Professional services cover accounting, investment banking, consulting, advertising and marketing, PR, legal and property-related services. There is heavy buying inertia: professional services partners work hard at building strong personal relationships with clients and clients are reluctant to switch once they've found somebody good. There is an "IBM syndrome" with premium services for board-level projects – no CEO or CFO ever got fired for hiring McKinsey or Goldman Sachs.

We can recognize that there is a value to long-standing professional services relationships. Strategy consultants, for example, take the initial two months of the first project for a new client just getting up to speed on the business. They then go on to give you a return on that investment in future projects. You don't want to pay for that learning curve too many times.

All true. But simply being seen to monitor and check the charges, and being willing to review them with the partners, can cut them by 10–20%. Partners really don't like discussing billing rates and project costs. They want their clients to love them dearly and they want to be seen to be doing everything possible to help the client out. Just putting the numbers on the table and sitting back looking disappointed can usually get you a good discount. (I'm not sure if this is true of the top investment banks. I have never won at poker with an I-banker.)

Make sure that the way the services firm is paid gives them an incentive to save you money. Don't pay advertising agencies a percentage of the advertising budget, or architects a percentage of project spend – do a rough sizing of the job, then agree a fixed fee. If you're buying a business in an M&A deal, don't pay your investment bank a percentage of transaction value – agree a base fee plus a bonus depending on how cheap you get it.

OUTSOURCING

Many businesses have outsourced the burden of people cost management in IT, accounting and HR, pushing it outside to firms like Accenture, IBM, EDS or PwC.

An outsourcing relationship is still a supplier relationship, but it is different in degree. You are much more locked in, either because the contract is longer term or because switching suppliers would be a huge practical hassle, or both. You have to manage a quasi-monopoly supplier.

A good analogy is the relationship between a regulator and a heavily regulated private-sector industry like water, airports, railways. You have to think and manage a bit like a regulator.

A regulator's toolkit is a good starting point for structuring and managing an outsourcing contract and I give an example overleaf.

One theme to consider under outsourcing is whether the optimization is single company or multifirm. Single-company optimization could in theory be achieved by the client firm itself, if it could overcome history and inertia. Stronger value can be created with multifirm optimization, where fixed costs are shared, there are economies of scale and scope and shared learning curves.

REGULATOR'S TOOLKIT

TOOL	COMMENTS	EXAMPLES
Pricing targets		Base price per unit of output must decline annually at RPI minus x
SLAs	Service level agreements	95% of trains will arrive or depart within 5 mins of schedule
KPIs	Key performance indicators (a bit like SLAs)	UK NHS: Nobody sits in A&E for more than four hours before being seen by a doctor
Investment expectations	Where, ballpark $$, how much recoupable in higher charges	A new airport terminal; a safety overhaul of railway signals
Profit margin and return on capital	Open-book access to firm's accounts	A water company with target ROC of 8%
Procedures in case of breach		Financial penalties for failing to deliver on SLAs and KPIs; withdrawal of license to operate
Renewal process	For renegotiating operating licenses at the next round in x years' time	

TRAVEL COSTS

Travel costs are non-trivial. For an on-the-road salesperson, executive, consultant or engineer, they can add 15–30% to total headcount cost. IBM, PwC and Accenture spend well over a billion dollars a year each on travel, split roughly $500m air, $300m hotel, $100m car rental and $100m other costs.

In the early 1990s this spend was pretty much unmanaged. Local offices or individual managers made their own choice of travel agent, maybe a friend of a friend. Agents were paid commission as a percentage of transaction value. Travel policies were rare and rarely enforced.

But in the mid-1990s big changes came to business travel. Airlines moved to eliminate commissions. Travel agents had to start charging fees, so their costs became much more transparent to their customers. This switch removed their incentive to sell higher fares and get a high commission.

Within corporations, the position of travel manager was created to oversee travel buying. Travel agency suppliers were consolidated from dozens to two or three, most likely Amex/Rosenbluth, Carlson or WTP/BTI. Principal agency contracts were now reviewed every three to five years. Travel managers could bypass their agencies and deal directly with airlines, hotels, GDSs, conference organizers.

A second wave of change came with the internet. Travel providers now encourage customers to book directly on their own websites, often offering web-only discounts. Several low-cost airlines, like Ryanair and easyJet in Europe, can only be booked direct, mainly online. Online agencies like Expedia and Opodo allow the end user to do most of what a travel agent does – search, book, pay – with more flexibility and lower cost.

Whereas the first wave of change had mainly affected big corporations, the second wave changed things for the SME (small and medium enterprise) market. SMEs grabbed the opportunity to save a bundle with online self-booking.

This revolution in travel management encapsulates well the supplier management themes of this chapter: fewer better suppliers, intelligent negotiation and understanding of supplier economics, introduction of professional procurement, a move to fixed-fee pricing. And it also serves to introduce the power of the internet as a lever for cost reduction, which we'll come back to in Chapter 7.

TRICKY COST IN MARKETING

Marketing costs are frustrating to analyze. Are you spending way too much or way too little? Why don't you just cut 20% everywhere, would the business suffer? Or why don't you invest ahead of competitors, take the high ground?

My personal inclination is to protect marketing spend. I worry about repeating the mistakes of the mid-1970s after the oil price crisis, when so many companies hacked advertising budgets and destroyed their brands.

You do need to check whether your marketing spend as a percentage of revenue is broadly where you'd expect it to be versus competitors. (It could be OK to be investing a higher percentage if you're trying to catch up with a larger player or defending a premium niche.) But your main focus should be on increasing productivity. Are you spending on the right channels and using the right media, to reach the right customer segments? Are you buying effectively?

Take IBM Global Services and Accenture. Both are selling outsourcing and consulting services to corporate buyers. Both do high-level B2B. Accenture's blanket poster coverage in major airports, along the moving walkways, is well targeted at the frequent flyer executive. But IBM's primetime television campaigns are quite likely to be unproductive – all those ad dollars when the target executives can only be a tiny percentage of the mass television audience.

The message it gives me is that IBM is a fat-cat organization that can afford to waste millions on useless marketing.

Another example: I was working with a technology firm in the US. Like all its competitors, the firm was spending millions of dollars every year on booths at technology conferences. It had never seen any payback on that investment. Meanwhile it was failing to get onto the vendor matrices produced by tech analyst firms like Gartner and Forrester. These were critical – if you weren't on the matrix then corporate buyers wouldn't even invite you to tender. The firm switched all the conference money into working with those tech analysts and it started seeing results.

Consumer businesses are also trying to make their marketing dollars work harder. They are shifting spend away from mainstream broadcast television and mass-market publications, toward narrower niche vehicles (specialist television, radio, magazines) and direct measurable-response marketing (online, coupons, telemarketing).

So you should protect marketing spend, but make it more productive.

HOW ABOUT IT?

In 2004 an article in the *Harvard Business Review*, by Nick Carr, claimed that "IT Doesn't Matter". Carr's argument was that IT is no longer a proprietary technology that can add strategic differentiated value to a business. It's now just another piece of open infrastructure, like electricity or office supplies, to be managed mainly to minimize its cost.

The article caused a ruckus in the IT community. Tech bosses rushed to defend the sexy strategic nature of IT, harping back to the glory days of Y2K and the dot-com boom when for a few years IT accounted for over 50% of all capital expenditure in North America.

I remember several years ago working on a big business turnaround. We had agreement on all the cost-reduction programs apart from IT. In its best years the business had only made about $100m operating profit, but the new CEO wanted to spend $400m on an IT revamp over three years, mainly on point-of-sale and accounting systems. The old systems were indeed clunky and out of date, but the CEO was unable to say how the IT investment was going to deliver any better sales or gross margins, or lower operating costs. It was a leap of faith in the value of having great top-end IT. It was already an outdated approach.

As an interesting modern contrast, take Google. Its search engine software embodies leading-edge proprietary technology. But Google takes a stripped-to-the-bone, no-frills approach to its back-end IT, its data centers and network operations. In the sense that Nick Carr means the phrase, even for Google IT doesn't matter.

In this new cost-centered IT environment, the priority is to drive for lower costs and higher productivity with minimum extra capex, cheaper commodity equipment and less complex and customized software. Avoid being an innovator, see what other firms are doing, copy what seems cheap and efficient. Expect annual budgets to go down not up.

The savings with this approach can be tremendous. I worked with a medium-sized sales and marketing business in the US that was about to install Siebel for $6m in license fees and at least the same again in deployment costs. We figured out we could patch together a good-enough CRM solution using a combination of Excel spreadsheets and Salesforce.com at a cost of around $100,000 a year. And we could get it up and running in six weeks, not six months. Now that's a cost saving.

The other key with IT is to break the cost down into meaningful pieces and look at it piece by piece. The pieces might be operations (hosting, network), maintenance, architecture and systems performance, small CRs (change requests) and real market/customer-driven development projects. Each piece has very different dynamics and decision criteria. Often managers think they're "investing" $100m a year in IT, when in reality 90% of the spend is on maintenance, operations and system infrastructure, rather than on real discretionary investment in next-generation functionality and client-facing applications.

REDUCING NON-LABOR OVERHEAD

A few years ago I ran a cost-reduction project for a pan-European business providing commercial services to airlines and airports. It had an infrastructure of depots, vehicles and equipment at over 20 of Europe's main airports. We had a nice simple framework for looking at non-labor overhead costs:

POTENTIAL SOURCE OF COST SAVING	APPLIED TO COST CATEGORIES

Vendor price
• Select, negotiate, retender
• Central purchasing
 	
Quantity
• Volume, usage
• Service frequencies, standards
• Substitute, eliminate
 	
Insource or outsource
 	
Property utilization
• Sublease
• Consolidate, dispose
 	
Management
• Line accountability
• Reporting
	• Property
	  o Lease cost
	  o Utilities
	  o Other (maintenance etc.)
	• Vehicles
	• Other equipment
	• IT & communication
	• Professional and financial services
	• Other costs (disposables etc.)

As an illustration take property maintenance. Almost all the potential sources of cost saving were applicable:

○ **Vendor price**: maintenance contracts hadn't been properly retendered for several years; and we could get better rates by consolidating purchasing with one vendor, at least within one country.

○ **Quantity**: We were maintaining properties too frequently and at too high a standard (with no health and safety implications of a reduction in that standard).

○ **Insource/outsource**: In some locations we still had in-house staff doing maintenance, at low utilization – it was better to outsource.

○ **Property utilization**: This was not relevant.

○ **Management**: This was very relevant – line accountability for maintenance costs floated somewhere between depot managers, head office procurement and head office property; in practice nobody really owned the area or pushed for efficiencies.

We went through every location applying the same checklist and at the end of a three-month process we had our target 15% saving.

There were some interesting cases of completely eliminating a cost. One big-ticket item was the provision and cleaning of uniforms for production and transport staff (over 5,000 people across Europe). The Swiss operation had this all meticulously outsourced, with detailed service level agreements, computerized laundry schedules and reordering, and other good things Swiss-style. The Spanish operation had negotiated years ago that employees would do their own uniform laundering at home in return for a better canteen lunch. We found an even cheaper solution: eliminate textile uniforms altogether and move to paper-based disposables.

Site insurance was another big ticket, with only one or two vendors interested in offering the type of cover we needed, so cover was expensive and we had a very high deductible. Looking at claims history and taking a hard look at real risk exposure, we eliminated insurance payments and became self-insured.

This approach could be called the Input–Factory–Output model. On the input side you can do less or not do something at all. In the factory you can employ different business models, more efficient processes and so on. On the output side you can set standards appropriately, for example a 24-hour not 4-hour response time.

COST MANAGERS: RYANAIR

Ryanair, headquartered in Dublin but with its biggest operational base at London Stansted, is one of the two major low-cost airlines in Europe; the other is easyJet. They are fierce competitors: Ryanair's first marketing statement on its website is "50% cheaper than easyJet".

Both companies took a lot of the low-cost airline concept from Southwest Airlines in the US, which was the low-cost pioneer back in the 1970s:

○ One plane type, with a fast turnaround, flying simple point-to-point routes.
○ One-class seating, no assigned seats.
○ No frilly services (e.g. no meals).
○ Cheaper distribution (e.g. avoid travel agents).
○ Cheaper ticketing and check-in.

But Ryanair has taken low cost to new extremes. It makes Southwest look like Singapore Airlines.

Ryanair's approach to cost is: why should we pay for anything? Or even better, why can't we turn cost into revenue?

Take airports. Airlines using Heathrow get hit with very high airport charges (landing fees, passenger and security charges and so on). It's the same for prime close-to-city-center airports in Germany, France, Sweden and so on. There's a lot of demand and a limited supply, so prices are high.

But dozens of secondary airports around Europe used to be barely used. Ryanair found that not only would those airports not charge it very much to land there, they might in many cases actually subsidize it to fly in, to help develop local jobs and tourism.

This has resulted in some creative airport nomenclatures. Stockholm Vasteras, for instance, is over 100km away from downtown Stockholm. But customers don't seem to mind when they are getting a London–Stockholm round trip for under £40. Ryanair is now the highest-volume carrier between the UK and Sweden.

With some of its new airports, where it is often the first sizeable carrier, Ryanair has single-handedly opened up a new set of destinations for tourism and for vacation home purchasing – like its flights from the UK to the south and west of Italy, or to Zaragoza and Santiago in Spain.

Or take distribution. Ryanair is now sold 99% on the Ryanair.com website. It developed its own internet booking engine for a minuscule investment. It doesn't sell through travel agents at all. If you contact the company by phone for any reason – a booking, change, cancellation – it's a premium-rate phone call. If you want to alter your flight, it's an £18.50 fee per person per one-way flight, plus any fare difference. A name change is £70, which is a pretty outrageous number. Airport check-in costs £3 per flight vs zero if you check in online. Do it yourself, please!

Payment charges reflect and recover Ryanair's processing cost – if you pay by debit card it's cheaper than a credit card. There are no tickets, just a printout of the internet booking confirmation.

So Ryanair's net distribution cost is probably close to zero. (Back in the late 1990s BA had a big campaign to reduce its distribution cost, which it then estimated at over 20% of revenue, its biggest single-line cost.)

Or take the actual passenger flight experience. Ryanair does all the obvious things like not providing free meals and drinks. But as in all other areas it goes that one step further. The airline hit the headlines for charging a passenger for a wheelchair at its London base, Stansted. The CEO was very comfortable defending the company's position in public. He argued that most airports provided wheelchairs for free, but BAA, the operator of Stansted airport, would have charged Ryanair £18 for a wheelchair, almost double the £10 each way that the passenger was paying for his actual flight to the south of France.

There are stories that Ryanair is considering removing headrests and armrests from seats because they break too often. Passengers are already charged for every piece of hold baggage, £6 for the first and £12 each for up to two additional checked bags, but they may soon be encouraged to travel with no baggage at all, so the planes can be turned round faster.

The cheaper-than-cheap attitude isn't just with customers. Staff have been told to stop charging their mobile phones at work as it costs the company 1p per charge for electricity.

These hard-core cheapskate stories and Scrooge-style outrages are great press fodder and generate massive PR and marketing for the airline at zero cost – another admirable aspect of the low-cost model.

The Ryanair philosophy, which has so far proved correct, is that passengers are happy to pay the lowest possible prices for a basic airline bus service. The only things passengers are really concerned about, apart from price, are safety and punctuality. On safety, Ryanair has (touch wood) as good a record as any airline, if not better. It is top of the list on punctuality, delivering 85% of on-time flights in 2007 (vs 70% for BA, according to AEA).

Finally, let's look at the bottom line. To year end March 2007 Ryanair's operating margin was 21% on an average scheduled revenue per passenger flight of €44. BA's was 7%, in a very good year for both BA and business travel, on an average revenue per passenger flight of over €300 and on a total revenue six times Ryanair's. Ryanair's margin is unheard of in the airline industry, even for Southwest (and it used to be 30%).

Toolkit – Suppliers

UNDERSTAND AND PLAY THE BALANCE OF POWER, IN PARTICULAR WHERE THERE IS:
- High interdependence.
- High buyer dependence.

MOVE TO FEWER SUPPLIERS
- And make your selection from better ones.

NEGOTIATE INTELLIGENTLY
- Understand suppliers' economics.
- Try to find win–wins.
- Leave profit for the supplier.
- Consolidate buying power.
- Trade off price and terms.

DON'T GET LOCKED IN
- Have one credible alternative.
- Reduce switching cost.
- Avoid long-term contracts.
- Maintain an active marketplace.

MANAGE TOTAL COST OF OWNERSHIP
- Not just up-front and obvious cost or capex, also ongoing and hidden costs.
- Factoring in the benefits of trialing and future flexibility.

GET TOUGH ON SERVICES COST
- Central procurement.
- Professional services.
- Outsourcing.
- Travel.

○ Marketing.
○ IT.

REDUCE NON-LABOR OVERHEAD

○ Vendor price.
○ Quantities and frequencies.
○ Insource or outsource.
○ Property utilization.
○ Management accountability and reporting.

6 Cost Cutting Case Study

In 2006 I did a classic cost-reduction program for the European division of a US-based business services company. The business had operations in most main European countries, including Turkey, with strong regional and country management structures as well as a central European head office. In Europe it had (by order of magnitude; I'm disguising the real figures) around $2 billion sales and 10,000 employees. To cover interest payments and start paying down debt, it needed to increase operating profit by an extra 4–5% of sales. Achieving this via revenue growth was not a realistic option, so a big chunk of cost had to be cut.

Management set up a project team, including outside consultants, and I was brought in to lead the process. It was a good comprehensive example of a cost-reduction exercise, not just the absolute and final results but also how it rolled through over a six-month timeframe.

Month 1

In the first month we worked mainly out of the head office on three key start-up activities.

We had to size the prize. We had a top-down financially driven target of 4% of sales, but we had to translate that into cost savings targets, in meaningful buckets of cost, and do a first-pass sanity check that those targets were at least feasible.

We broke the costs down into five categories:

O Direct labor
O Direct materials
O Indirect (overhead) labor
O Indirect non-labor costs – property leases
O Indirect non-labor costs – all other

Direct costs, both labor and materials, were the direct-line costs associated with delivery of the business services. They were going to be the toughest to address, since they were the bread-and-butter activities of the business and were under constant day-to-day scrutiny, with line managers always looking for ways to save a dollar here and a dollar there. So although these were by far the biggest cost buckets, we had to be prudently conservative in assuming any extra savings from the cost program.

Indirect labor represented the staff costs of all support and overhead functions – mainly SG&A (sales, general and admin) activities but also some indirect operational activities, like facilities maintenance. It also could include some layers of operational management, supervision and line support. (We'll come back to definitional integrity in a moment.)

Indirect non-labor represented all the non-labor cost except direct materials. The big categories were property, property-related costs (like utilities and maintenance), equipment, IT and communications and professional services. We ended up breaking out property as a separate line as it was such a big chunk and we had much less chance of achieving big short-term savings.

Once we had this breakdown (which took about two weeks of number crunching with the central finance team) we took another pass at our target savings, which are listed opposite.

Our biggest percentage savings target was in indirect labor. The country and regional operations all had very different SG&A structures, built up via acquisitions over the last 20 years, which had never been reviewed in a consolidated way and had (mainly) been

SIZING THE PRIZE, MONTH 1	Current % of sales	Target saving %	Weighted saving %
Direct labor	40	3	1.2
Direct materials	20	3	0.6
Indirect labor	10	15	1.5
Indirect non-labor – property	15	5	0.8
Indirect non-labor – other	10	10	1.0
TOTAL	95		5.1

left decentralized. We were cautious about our ability to get short-term savings in property leases, so we targeted only 5% (this turned out to be optimistic). And we thought that a concentrated focus on the other indirect costs, like maintenance, equipment and external services, should yield good results because they often slipped below management's radar, so we set a 10% target. In the direct cost categories we thought we could target a 3% extra saving.

When we added up our sanity-checked sizings, weighting our targets by the percentage of sales represented by each cost category, it came to just over 5% of sales. So even with 20% slippage we could hit 4% of sales, the minimum financial goal.

When we sized the prize, we were defining the targets as savings that could be being achieved at a full run rate in (at the latest) six months' time. ("Run rate" means the full annualized financial impact once everything is up and running. So for example I might see only a $1m improvement in the first financial year as benefits ramp up and there are offsetting costs of change, but I could exit the year at a full run rate of $2m.) So if we thought we could get out of a nasty property lease but not for at least two years, that was certainly interesting and the property department should be working on it, but it would not help us on this cost program. We were not including any one-off investments needed to get the costs out, like contract buyouts or redundancy costs; these would be captured in a separate investment budget.

In Month 1 we also began to build a good central database. We knew that one way to tease out cost savings would be to benchmark internal best practice across the over 50 operating units and over 20 regional or country offices across Europe. To do that benchmarking we had to have a robust, apples-to-apples database that allowed us to compare different approaches and productivities. The database had to be good enough for local managers to accept that benchmarking was accurate and comparable. This was most important in the case of indirect labor, where the value of benchmarking was going to be greatest – not around dollar cost, which would vary with wage rates, but headcount.

So through Month 1, working from head office by phone with the local operations, we built a detailed indirect labor database. By the end of the month we were 99% certain we were comparing similar activities, even if the terms and definitions varied wildly. This process quickly eliminated some wrong interpretations of old, unscrubbed numbers. For example, head office was convinced that Turkey and Spain were hugely overstaffed in their support functions. The database showed that Turkey and Spain included in-house facilities staff (cleaners, maintenance, canteen) in their headcounts, while most northern European operations had outsourced those activities, getting the headcount off their payroll (but not the cost off their P&Ls).

Our last main task in Month 1 was to get top management to buy into the process and the targets. We held a working session at the end of the month with the top half dozen European divisional managers from head office plus the line managers of the dozen or so main country or regional operations. We put up our sizing of the prize and went through the first results of our database, comparing productivity and cost across operating units.

Our main objective was to get the line managers to leave the meeting seeing the process and targets as their own, not an imposed head office initiative or a here-we-go-again consulting exercise. We then worked through the process needed over the next several months to get to the target run-rate saving.

To recap:

MONTH 1: KEY ACTIVITIES
○ Size and sanity check the prize.
○ Build a good central database.
○ Get top management to buy into the process and the targets.

Month 2

In Month 2 we shifted the focus of work out from the center into the operating units; in this case out into the region and country organizations.

Each regional or country general manager now had a month to come up with plans to get the cost savings in his or her unit. The central project team was available to assist if requested. Otherwise, the central team focused on centrally managed overhead costs like corporate insurance, IT architecture, and central finance and HR.

We also set up a tracking system to be ready to go live at the end of the month. A good tracker is an essential element of any cost program. Without it cost savings seem to vanish, or turn out to be much smaller than first claimed. Or six months later you find they are still not implemented. Or you get the cost waterbed effect: you press down hard on one side and another bunch of costs springs up behind your back, as managers slide costs around between budgets.

A tracker takes all the cost-saving ideas and initiatives that get generated and lets you see their status:

○ Identified
○ Line management committed
○ Actioned
○ Run rate achieved

123

As an example, take an initiative to combine two small distribution facilities into one unit:

○ This is **identified** via working sessions and some financial operational analysis. A first-cut sizing says we could save $2.4m runrate annual cost for a one-time cost (mainly getting out of one lease and a redundancy program) of $1m. Local management has been involved and sanity checked the idea, so it is already more than just a vague, top-of-head possibility. At this stage it can go into the tracker as identified.

○ The next stage is to get **line management committed**. If the idea involved two facilities in Germany, this would occur when the general manager for Germany has signed off on both the concept and the target savings number. If the facilities had a functional line manager, like a head of logistics, then he or she would need to sign off as well. At this point a line manager fully owns the initiative and is committed to implementing it.

○ The next stage is when the key elements of the initiative have been **actioned**. Here that might mean that notice has been given on the lease, personnel changes and redundancies have been communicated and negotiated, and a timetable has been set for consolidation, with plans in place for stock reallocation and transport rescheduling.

○ The last stage is when you can clearly see target **run rate achieved** in the monthly management accounts. In this example, that is when distribution costs are coming in at $200,000 a month below previous (or budget) levels. Until you get to this point, the initiative is still outstanding in the tracker.

Major slippage can occur between any of these stages: in savings, in timeframe or both. A good tracker maintains visibility, pressure and transparency.

Trackers must count £ or $ and also, very importantly, headcount. Headcount is where the biggest slippage can occur – and where the risk of a cost waterbed is greatest. Trackers must also adjust for changes in business volume and revenue, where these drive variable costs. For example, if sales go up 5% we might expect direct materials cost to go up 5%; so when direct materials increase by only 2%, that is really a 3% cost saving.

A common debate is whether savings should be measured versus budget or versus actual starting point (assuming this is, as it usually is, lower than budget). This can sound arcane to outsiders but is deeply emotional for managers. An outsider might assume that actual starting point is the most logical measure: it is easier to track and it represents the actual condition of the business before cost cutting. But line managers will have fought their corner hard in the last annual budget round. They will want to claim any savings versus budget as real savings, reflecting real tough choices. I think they have a point and I will accept budget as the baseline.

At the end of Month 2 we reconvened the top management group. The purpose was to agree low-hanging fruit and identify tough high-hanging nuts.

Each line manager came back with a first pass at where they had found savings opportunities. In some geographies the targets had been met or exceeded, in others there had been little or no result. Likewise if we cut the costs and savings by functional area there were good opportunities in direct cost, but not so much, or not so consistently, in indirect cost.

Where savings were already promising and well identified, implementation became the full responsibility of the line manager, with progress to be measured and monitored centrally via our tracker system.

Where we had big shortfalls versus what was needed, the tough nuts to crack, our central project team would go in over the next one or two months to work alongside local line management. If the

BUDGETS AND COST CUTTING: THE MANAGER'S DILEMMA

Cost-cutting programs give sadistic CEOs and CFOs endless pleasurable ways to twist the knife into line managers. One of the most fun is the "so why wasn't this in the budget?" attack.

Say MultiGlom Inc. has just launched a cost-cutting program only a few months after the annual budget process. Unit manager Bill comes to the first CEO review with a proposal for a 5% headcount cut versus budget.

"Bill," purrs the CEO, "I'm impressed. But how come this wasn't in the budget? Was your budget padded?"

"No, urk, not padded, aark," croaks Bill.

The CFO is licking his lips. "I'm sensing padding. I think this should have been in the budget."

The CEO agrees. "Bill, I think you need to put this back into the budget, that's your base case. Now what we're really looking for is 5% over and above that. And I'm not seeing anything yet. Any thoughts?"

Poor Bill has had the knife slid up his sphincter. (Kay's up next, and she's just decided to say she can't find any savings.)

It's a bit like Catch 22: you can only get out of combat duty if you're mad, and if you want to get out of combat duty you can't be mad. Or like the old ducking-stool test: if you drowned you weren't a witch.

blockages were real, we needed to see if there were any new ways of coming at the savings. If the blockages were a problem of management, we needed to find that out as soon as possible and either change the mindset or change the leadership.

So at the end of Month 2 we already had a tracker that, at the top level, looked like the one opposite (numbers are not real). I'm using two regions as an illustration of differences; in reality there were many more regions.

TRACKER SUMMARY, END MONTH 2 €M	Target saving	Identified	Committed	Actioned	Achieved run rate
Region 1					
Direct labor	6.0	5.0	5.0	2.0	1.0
Direct materials	3.0	3.0	3.0	1.5	1.0
Indirect labor	7.0	5.0	5.0	1.0	0.5
Indirect non-labor – property	4.0	1.0	1.0		
Indirect non-labor – other	5.0	4.0	4.0	1.0	0.5
TOTAL	25.0	18.0	18.0	5.5	3.0
% of target		72%	72%	22%	12%
Region 2					
Direct labor	9.0	5.0	3.0		
Direct materials	4.5	3.0	2.0		
Indirect labor	10.5	1.0	0.5		
Indirect non-labor – property	6.0	0.5	0.5		
Indirect non-labor – other	7.5	1.5	0.5		
TOTAL	37.5	11.0	6.5	0.0	0.0
% of target		29%	17%	0%	0%
Regions 3, 4, 5 ...					

We can see that Region 1 has pretty much come up with the goods. The regional GM (general manager) has already identified savings that would come to over 70% of the initial targets. And she has already committed herself to those savings, this is no "provisional" estimate that she needs to take another month to sign off. There is a good chance she will get to 80% with one more push. The only area of big shortfall is in property, so the central team might need to send in a property expert to help. Apart from that there's no need for central team involvement, as long as the GM now moves hard and fast into implementation.

Region 2 is a different kettle of fish. Identified savings are modest, under 30% of target. And the GM is not yet fully committing to even those identified savings. He has identified almost no possible savings in indirect costs. So this region represents a real challenge. The central project team needs to go in and work intensively with local management for the next two months.

It is reasonable to expect already to see run-rate savings at more than 15% of target by the end of Month 2. Some low-hanging fruit will have been picked, including agreements not to fill open positions that were in the budget to be filled and getting some quick wins with suppliers.

MONTH 2: KEY ACTIVITIES

O Move out from the center into operating units.

O Set up a tracking system.

O Agree low-hanging fruit and identify tough high-hanging nuts.

O Run-rate savings at least 15–20% of target by the end of the month.

INHERENT CONTRADICTIONS

You could challenge whether strategy consultants, given their natural habitat of five-star hotel offsites, gourmet restaurants and flat-bed air travel, can have anything to say about cost management or be involved in any cost-reduction projects. This is a fair challenge. In my defense I could honestly say I am a real cheapskate with my clients' expenses, and it would be true, but you probably wouldn't believe me.

My publisher raised this point with some relish and showed me an Alex cartoon strip from the UK's *Daily Telegraph*, where two pin-striped London execs from GlobalMegaBank are gossiping:

Exec 1: So, this new cost-cutting officer... the bank is *paying* him a million dollars a year to *save* money?

Exec 2: It may seem odd to us, Clive, but this is the American way of doing business and we have to respect it...

Exec 1: So you reckon this new guy is a Yank?

Exec 2: I expect so... frankly if you want a job like this done efficiently and single-mindedly, it's about possessing certain key qualities... and Americans tend to be very blessed that way...

Exec 1: Absence of a sense of irony?

Exec 2: Quite. At least this chap won't be impeded by awareness of the inherent contradiction in his role...

Month 3

In Month 3 the special project team focused on tackling the tough nuts, leaving the regions and functions that were making good progress on their own to carry on their good work.

In this case the main tough nut was the operation in Germany. The GM there had been handed a big share of target overall savings and had come back to the end-of-Month-2 review session (reporting to his European CEO and the private equity partner) saying that he couldn't find any savings at all. This didn't go down well. After some one-on-one stomping sessions he invited the special project team to parachute in and help. So we put on our winter overcoats (this was January) and headed for Frankfurt.

We eventually got about 60% of the German target. Squeezing out that result was a classic example of how tenacity is all in cost cutting. In every meeting and on every topic we were stonewalled by local management at least three times before we got any movement. At first rather pleasantly, via long, companionable and discursive dinners with some good wine; and then later, in an in-your-face way, as in all-day "brainstorms" in rooms with windows left open in an outside temperature of –5 degrees, snow blowing in, as the management team chainsmoked in baleful silence. We once flew in especially for a meeting that they had scheduled, only to sit in an empty meeting room all day while they had to deal with an "unexpected crisis".

My trusted consultant colleague Barbara, herself of implacable Teutonic stock and true grit, became heroic in her persistence. Frozen out, shouted at, given no information, patronized, she ploughed on and got the savings. Stranded overnight at least once a week in fog-bound, ice-gripped Frankfurt airport, she would be back at the offices next morning, 7 a.m. sharp, pinning the customer service manager against her desk, pointing out that German customer service productivity was half that of other regions and here were five ideas on how to close the gap. In the end even the local team was won over and just had to start cooperating. (Barbara revealed when she'd almost finished the job that she was very pregnant, in fact birth was now imminent. The locals had assumed she was overeating to deal with the stress.)

Month 3 is also the time to check there are no false trails being pursued. We had a good example in this case, the Europe CFO's plan to pull together finance functions that were now decentralized across multiple regions or countries into one center for Europe. The logic seemed reasonable and obvious: economies of scale in most activities, including in management overheads. But there were big one-time costs involved for relocating people and offices, and in particular for consolidating systems onto a common SAP platform.

Ah, SAP, that anathema for true blue cost cutters! SAP is a CFO's wet dream. All possible enterprise data, in a 100% consistent format across business units and geographies and functions, updated daily or even to the minute, with enough metrics and drilldowns and consolidations and reports to satisfy even Robert McNamara. SAP's ERP (enterprise resource planning) business, with its roots in German corporate accounting and its presence in 80% of the Fortune 500, is the only non-American business to be a global leader in a large software market.

SAP has a sort of force-of-nature momentum that seems unstoppable, so it is almost pointless in most large corporations raising the pitiful question: "Why are we doing this?" But the reality is, it's usually far from clear why SAP is going in and it's very unclear what if any will be the benefits, apart from the CFO knowing the numbers a few days earlier. In three cases where I have been working closely with a company doing a major SAP deployment, I saw little or no benefit in lower cost or in better decision making and control. The extra costs of SAP itself are very large, not only one time but also annual going forward; not just the money to SAP but also the huge suck-up of management time. And it normally takes years.

So in our case study, SAP was raising its ugly head because the US head office wanted it and the Europe CFO was an enthusiast. In the middle of an aggressive cost-reduction project we were suddenly looking at a huge cost add-back – oh, and to cap it all, they were proposing using Accenture to manage the deployment, SAP's common collaborator on the cost front.

SAP was being cost justified as the enabler of finance centralization. Let's say there were 500 finance staff across Europe in over a dozen locations. The SAP-championing analysis had said that this could be cut to 400 with a common system. Bingo, with a 20% saving SAP pays back in under two years.

But by looking just at tactical efficiencies, including best practice across offices and changing some back-office processes, we had come up with a bigger savings opportunity, about 25%, without having to change and consolidate ERP systems. Any further gains from also deploying SAP would be modest at best – even the CFO champion couldn't argue for more than an extra 5–10% and at that level there was no investment case. And if we started putting SAP in we would have to delay getting the tactical cost savings, because we needed the extra staff kept on through the deployment phase for up to two years.

Although our main focus in Month 3 was on tackling the tough nuts, we also had to make sure that the managers who'd started well had maintained their momentum. Were they moving strongly from ideas and analysis into implementation?

By the end of Month 3 we should have been seeing all supplier changes identified and negotiations begun, with about 50% finished. If we saw situations where these opportunities were still at the ideas stage, we'd get slippage. Managers needed to have sat down face to face to negotiate better terms or to have begun the process of finding alternative suppliers. A good percentage, say 50%, of these supplier changes needed to be completed and the run-rate benefits already flowing through the P&L.

COST-CUTTING KIWIS

I am pretty handy myself at management-speak, but my two main clients on this project, the European CEO and COO, were in a different buzzword league. (They were both Antipodeans and these work best with a Kiwi/Ozzie drawl.) Let's call them Bill and Ted.

Bill: "So Ted, where are we on savings, grossimodo?"

Ted: "We still need a rack and stack, but we've got line of sight on $20m. Nothing yet on property in Germany, but Andrew's doing a deep dive right now."

Bill: "Yep, yep. Need to get cracking. Deep dive, rack and stack, OK then, let's lock and load, asap."

Ted: "Two weeks grossimodo, max."

It's surprising how quickly one absorbs the lingo. Within a few weeks I was locking and loading like an old hand.

Incidentally, my favorite bizspeak ever is what traders call it when the stock market drops badly, then recovers briefly for a bit, then resumes dropping. The short-lived recovery is a dead cat bounce.

The toughest nut in supplier renegotiations is trying to reduce property lease cost: either getting the rent down or getting out of redundant properties. We had about 20% excess property capacity across Europe, mainly in Germany plus a very large and expensive facility in Switzerland. Most leases still had three or more years to run, a few had over 10 years. These situations have to be attacked creatively, case by case. We had to put some real credible pressure on the landlord, like threatening to pull out of other properties, or going to arbitration, or stopping maintenance payments on shared sites. We had to look for possible win–wins where we could work with the landlord, like restructuring a site to increase value or finding subtenants. And we had to look creatively at financing and cash flow – the landlord may have different cash-flow requirements than us and prefer more money now in return for releasing us from a lease, or vice versa, lowering the rent in return for extending a tenancy.

Let's get back to momentum. Headcount reductions always take longer to identify and action because they are more painful and because of the need for proper process. But by end of Month 3, we needed to see all people reductions identified and discussions begun with individuals on timing and compensation.

Our last action in Month 3 was to reconvene the management group again for our end-of-month status review. Overall we were seeing a big jump in run-rate savings, up to 40%+ of target by the end of Month 3, pretty much in line with what we were hoping for.

MONTH 3: KEY ACTIVITIES
O Tackle the tough nuts.
O Eliminate false trails.
O Supplier negotiations/changes – all identified and begun, about 50% finished.
O People reductions – all identified and communicated and negotiations begun, vacant positions not filled, some early departures.
O Run-rate savings at least 40% of target by the end of the month.

Month 4

Month 4 is crunch-and-consolidate month, by which time most cost programs should be completed. The focus is on fixing slippages and underdelivering areas. The work is necessarily ad hoc.

Let's go straight to the end-of-month management meeting and see where we are on the tracker (see page 136). It shows a pretty good situation.

EUROPEAN LABOR MARKETS

How sticky labor cost is, and how expensive it is to sort out, depends a lot on which country you are operating in, particularly in Europe.

The UK is only slightly stickier than the very flexible US. In the private sector, dealing with salaried staff, you can usually assume that you can act freely and quickly based on a need to improve business profitability or to deal with non-performers. Three to six months' notice and redundancy cost would be a reasonable assumption.

There is one Western European labor market that is even more flexible than the UK or the US and it's a surprising one: Switzerland. Notice and redundancy terms in Switzerland can be even shorter and there is no expectation of any job security, particularly in white-collar jobs. The Swiss labor market is like that partly because unemployment is at 3–4%, i.e. basically zero. If you get fired you can be sure of getting another job quickly. The same is true, generally, in the US and the UK, at least in the last decade. So you get a virtuous loop of low unemployment and labor flexibility.

The same cannot be said of most other Western European labor markets. At the other end of the spectrum would be France, where job protection is so strong that the thought of hiring a new worker can make a business owner wake up sweating at 3 a.m. The moment you hire in France you have made a long-term capital commitment. In any significant pan-European cost-reduction program, the safest assumption to make is that you won't be able to reduce headcount in France in less than two years, if at all. The government will intervene in minor downsizings. If you act anyway because the French operation is haemorrhaging money, you'll be put in jail if you set foot in France. It is of course no wonder that French unemploy-

ment stays high, close to 10%, even when the economy is strong –
and that unemployment among young people runs at 20% plus, or
50% in the car-burning suburbs north of Paris.

Other Western European markets are somewhere between the
UK and France. You can restructure and get headcount reductions
but it can be very expensive and you have to go through lengthy
processes.

Redundancy cost often ratchets up with seniority, so if a problem
has been ducked for many years, finally sorting it out is really costly.
I once worked on restructuring a national soft drinks operation in
Spain. The biggest cost was a fleet of thousands of vehicles and
drivers delivering drinks to tens of thousands of mom-and-pop bars
and grocery stores. (There are said to be more bars on the Gran Via
in Madrid than in the whole of Norway.) This had once been very
profitable, but now multiple supermarkets were killing the independent grocers and the number of small bars was declining. The delivery network, which had been a great asset, was becoming a liability.
But the van drivers had been with the business for 10, 20, 30 years.
Average redundancy cost would have been two years' salary, so
management ducked it. When we got involved average redundancy
cost had gone up to three years' salary, which is a BIG NUMBER.
This time the company bit the bullet (well, half the bullet).

Eastern European labor markets like Poland and Hungary are at
an interesting crossroads. They come from a recent past of communism and "full" (even if fake) employment. Now their markets have
opened up they have had to deal with revealed unemployment and
scary social change. But they admire Anglo-Saxon capitalism and
flexibility more than EU paternalism and job protection. Their labor
markets now are an eccentric mix of flexibility and rigidity.

COST CUTTING CASE STUDY

TRACKER SUMMARY, END MONTH 4

€m	Target saving	Identified	Committed	Actioned	Achieved run rate
Region 1					
Direct labor	6.0	6.0	6.0	6.0	1.0
Direct materials	3.0	3.0	3.0	3.0	1.0
Indirect labor	7.0	6.0	6.0	6.0	0.5
Indirect non-labor – property	4.0	2.5	2.5	2.0	1.5
Indirect non-labor – other	5.0	5.0	5.0	4.5	0.5
TOTAL	25.0	22.5	22.5	21.5	3.0
% of target		90%	90%	86%	12%
Region 2					
Direct labor	9.0	7.5	7.5	6.5	6.5
Direct materials	4.5	4.0	4.0	4.0	4.0
Indirect labor	10.5	8.0	8.0	6.5	5.5
Indirect non-labor – property	6.0	2.0	2.0	1.5	1.0
Indirect non-labor – other	7.5	5.0	5.0	4.0	3.5
TOTAL	37.5	26.5	26.5	22.5	20.5
% of target		71%	71%	60%	55%

Regions 3, 4, 5 ...

Region 1, which started well, has continued to deliver. Identified savings are at 90% of target – and since we were only banking on 80% achievement overall, that's fine. All identified savings are fully committed, almost all have been actioned, and almost all of those have already been converted into run-rate savings, at 80% of target. The only cost area where this region has had trouble is property: only $2.5m savings have been identified versus a $4m target and we've only managed to achieve a run rate so far of $1m.

Region 2 started very slowly but, with help and push from the special project team, has closed a big chunk of the gap. Identified savings are at 70% of target and they've all been committed to – a big step forward for the reluctant regional GM. Because we got traction late in Region 2, there's still a drop-off when we move on to actioned savings and run rate, with run rate still only 55% of target. Again, property cost is the big shortfall. We were confident we could get run rate up to the 70% commitment in the next month. We had to decide whether it was worthwhile having one more push at property cost or whether we were banging our heads against a wall.

136

HOW LONG SHOULD A COST-REDUCTION PROGRAM TAKE?

In truly dire situations, where a business is making big losses and in the extreme case of bankruptcy and Chapter 11, you can cut costs very fast and very aggressively. In these situations you can confront bigger and stickier cost issues much harder than in business-as-usual conditions. Landlords can see there is a real risk of no rent getting paid. Employees (and government regulators, where they could intervene in labor disputes) can accept the need for rapid downsizing and even pay reductions and changes in working practice. You can achieve in weeks what could take years without a crisis. Older airlines in America now regularly go into Chapter 11 as the only way to negotiate with their expensive unionized workforce.

Outside an extreme crisis, it is hard to act at that pace. You need to bring your organization along with you, so that it accepts and even actively supports the need for change. You need to make the case and go through what is seen to be a reasonably thoughtful process of analysis, consultation and teamwork. This means that most special cost-reduction programs (something more than regular ongoing pruning) will take three to six months from kick-off to full run-rate savings. Any more than six months sounds like prevarication or plain bad management.

The public sector often announces cost-saving programs that will take years, as in: "We will cut the number of civil servants by 15% over the next five years." Well, nobody will track that over five years, the numbers will vanish into the ether and the minister responsible will change jobs three times. Even the most lovely-to-work-for organizations have natural attrition of at least 3%, so this goal could be achieved by just not hiring anybody, it wouldn't require you to take nasty decisions like getting rid of underperformers and overstaffed areas.

The BBC bizarrely announced a big cost-cutting program in 2005 that it said would be implemented over years – even the first stages

137

were not going to be implemented for at least six months while the broadcaster went through an enormous consultation process. The announcement of this unusually ambitious and long-term cost-cutting program strangely and happily coincided with the BBC's periodic negotiation with the UK government over its license fee funding.

Most highly successful private equity firms are big advocates and users of consultants in cost-cutting programs. All the top 10 private equity firms in Europe regularly use Bain, OC&C, McKinsey and the like. They think that consultants can speed things up and give management useful leverage. And cost cutting is one key way in which they extract value in their deals.

On the other hand, I know of lots of cases of very bad results from using consultants: bad analysis, bad conclusions, slow processes, high consulting costs and poor benefits. But only good clients get good consulting. In most cases the clients were at least as much to blame as the consultants. They had not defined the problem and task properly, or not managed the consultants to tight deadlines on tight activities. Good consulting requires good clients.

Overall, most regions were looking like Region 1 so we were on track overall, with run-rate savings up to 70%+ of target by the end of Month 4 and with confident line of sight on 80%+ within the next two months. (You see it's insidious, "line of sight" just slipped out, nice and natural.)

Let's summarize key activities over a three- to six-month cost-reduction program:

MONTH 1
O Size and sanity check the prize.
O Build a good central database.
O Get top management to buy into the process and the targets.

MONTH 2

○ Move out from the center into operating units.

○ Set up a tracking system.

○ Agree low-hanging fruit and identify tough high-hanging nuts.

○ Run-rate savings at least 15–20% of target by the end of the month.

MONTH 3

○ Tackle the tough nuts.

○ Eliminate false trails.

○ Supplier negotiations/changes – all identified and begun, about 50% finished.

○ People reductions – all identified and communicated and negotiations begun, vacant positions not filled, some early departures.

○ Run-rate savings at least 40% of target by the end of the month.

MONTH 4

○ Crunch and consolidate.

○ Fix slippages and underdelivering areas.

○ Run-rate savings at least 65–70% of target by the end of the month.

○ Line of sight on balance needed to get to 80% of target as soon as possible.

7

Wired and Global

The two key themes of the internet and globalization are very much of our time and are central to strategic cost management.

The Internet

Is it a fact or have I dreamt it, that by means of electricity, the world of matter has become a great nerve, vibrating thousands of miles in a breathless point of time?

—Nathaniel Hawthorne, 1851

A century ago, productivity in manufacturing was transformed by the development of mass production lines like Ford's. The internet has given us the opportunity for a similar productivity revolution in service businesses and functions.

Take a retail banking transaction. In a traditional bank branch this might cost on average \$15–20, including the costs of counter staff, office managers, buildings, documentation, cash handling and so on. Using phone and mail we might get this cost down to \$5–10, mainly by losing expensive high-street real estate. Using the internet we can cut cost to \$1 or less, even if we provide email or instant messaging support. The internet has enabled us to cut transaction cost by over 90%.

And the customer has a much better experience. No waiting in line in the branch or being on hold for 15 minutes. Instant access to information like account details or product rates. Being able to do the transaction at any time of day or night.

The internet has taken five things that used to be very expensive and time consuming (or maybe just impossible) and turned them into things that can be done at close to zero marginal cost with close to zero time delay:

○ Over the internet you can distribute **content** (text, data, images, audio, video) as a provider, and access it as a user, almost instantly for almost nothing. You can archive it in huge quantities in central servers or in personal devices. You can search billions of bytes of archive data comprehensively any time you want. You can edit and reformat painlessly. Any bedroom blogger can be an instant global publisher.

○ Email was the web's initial killer app and **communication** remains its core revolutionary value. A whole new repertoire has been created: email, instant messaging, voice-over-internet, WebEx meetings. All with zero marginal cost and zero time lag.

○ As we saw with retail banking, the internet can transform the cost and customer experience in any sales or service **transaction** – any process that involves selection, purchase, payment, changes and returns, advice, statements.

○ The internet also allows a business to exploit the benefits of **personalization**, to customize sales and service to an individual customer – like Amazon, with its personal shopping recommendations and cross-reference selling ("Other customers who bought x also bought y"). For the marketing department this is the holy grail, being able to target the "segment of one". The cost and time of sorting and accessing a customer database, and of tailoring and delivering a personal proposition, have reduced to close to zero.

○ And the internet has given the smallest niche business in the most remote corner of the globe to ability to **reach** any customer anywhere. Sitting in South London I can put "b&b Ulan Bator Mongolia" into Google, and 10 seconds later I am sending an email to the very nice-looking Idre Guesthouse, Sukhbaatar 5th Street, $4 per night, contact Tsetsegdelger Sumiya. This is the death of distance.

THE INTERNET AS A STRATEGIC COST-REDUCTION PROGRAM

The internet offers the opportunity to reduce cost in every nook and cranny of a business. While the overall prize is huge, each individual opportunity may be quite small and the opportunities will be scattered across every business function and customer segment. To maintain focus and scope you may need a special project team, reporting to top management, working against a framework like this:

FUNCTIONS	SUPPLIERS	EMPLOYEES	INTERACTIONS WITH CUSTOMERS	PROSPECTS	OTHERS
Production					
Purchasing					
Logistics					
R&D					
Marketing					
Sales					
Service					
HR					
Finance					

Across the top of the matrix structure your analysis around interactions, which is the internet's core transformational value. Matrix that against a list of top managers, to be comprehensive in coverage and to end up with concrete action programs attached to individual manager names. The list of these functions depends on the type of business. Under "others" you might find shareholders and stock analysts, regulators, trade press and market analysts. For a public-sector organization you might replace "customers" with voters, patients, constituents, claimants, taxpayers.

Sticking with the example, within marketing the main cost opportunities could be:

○ Move all brochures online – eliminate brochure mailings.
○ Switch ad spend toward search engines and affinity websites.
○ Set up online customer conferences and customer surveys.
○ Merge the website and sales collateral.
○ Move media buying onto a B2B exchange.
○ Create a news feed to PR agencies.

Within service:

○ Develop website self-help for product manuals and technical support.
○ Enable customers to deal directly with field engineers and delivery vehicles (like FedEx), including checking visit and delivery status online.

Within HR and finance:

○ Create paperless records – CVs, appraisals, payroll, accounting, billing.
○ Develop an online jobs marketplace – internal, external.
○ Use the intranet for internal communications.
○ Move all investor relations documentation and interaction online.
○ Do spot buying of short-term financing and cash deposits.

Putting those examples into our matrix gives the one filled in opposite.

Are these kinds of opportunities just about the internet? Aren't they about IT and technology defined much more broadly? Well yes, but... Computing power by itself is necessary but not sufficient:

| | | | INTERACTIONS WITH | | |
MANAGERS	SUPPLIERS	EMPLOYEES	CUSTOMERS	PROSPECTS	OTHERS
Marketing	B2B exchange (media)	Sales collateral	Conferences, surveys	Brochures, ad spend	PR news feed
Service			Self-help, scheduling		
HR	Jobs marketplace	Records, jobs marketplace			
Finance	Spot buying (debt, cash)	Records, payroll	Billing		Investor relations

look at the limited productivity gains in services in the 1970s and 1980s, post-computing but pre-internet. A services productivity revolution needs computing power plus reach and interactivity.

As well as creating radical opportunities to drive down cost, the internet creates tremendous downward pressure on prices: buyers can easily access better price information from a wider range of suppliers, some of whom may be willing to sell at marginal cost. Most of the cost saving tends to get passed on to customers.

Take airlines again. Pre-internet, you used to pay the same for an airline ticket whether you bought it through a travel agent or direct. Airlines had to pay the travel agents a commission out of that price, but didn't mind too much because the cost of a sale via their own sales branches or call centers wasn't much lower. When the internet arrived airlines had the option of taking a booking online direct from the passenger, at 5–10% of the cost of selling via an agent. Any gain in airline profitability was very short-lived, however, as soon consumers paid less if they booked online.

So the net result of the internet revolution is unlikely to be higher profitability. Instead it's a question of competitive survival. If you don't cut cost and pass on price reductions, you'll lose out to competitors who do.

The public sector, which mainly delivers labor-intensive services, could get huge productivity gains from the internet and give its customers a better service experience, in areas such as:

○ Tax and benefit administration – internal back-office processes, external interactions with taxpayers and recipients.

○ Health services – communication and data exchange among health practitioners, patient records, purchasing, capacity and resource sharing, back-office processing, staff admin, patient self-diagnosis and treatment.

○ Education – student applications and records, course marketing and clearing, general admin.

○ Local government – permits, penalties, planning applications, vendor procurement.

These are such big opportunities. The benefits need to be ground out step by step, with political will and persistence and with strong operational management. We'll come back to this topic in Chapter 10.

COST MANAGERS: INTERNET REVOLUTIONARIES

The internet is of course far from being just a cost tool. It is a creator and transformer of businesses and industries.

In the **interaction** category the big high-profile successes are new e-businesses. eBay created its own giant category, Monster dominates the e-jobs marketplace, PartyGaming is the world's largest poker room. Facebook and MySpace have transformed teenage socializing. Skype is driving the cost of international phone calls to zero.

Under **content** the mega-winner is Google, in a business category that didn't exist pre-internet. Old-economy content businesses like music publishers have been losers. Other earlier new ebiz winners, like AOL and Yahoo!, are getting killed by Google.

Under **retail** there are old businesses that have embraced the internet as one more distribution channel, like Wal-Mart and Tesco or Gap and Next. And there are old businesses that have made a

INTERNET REVOLUTIONS
(end-user businesses, not technology)

			EXAMPLES From pre-net era	New eBiz
Interaction	Comms: email, IM, VOIP			Hotmail, MSN, Skype
	Betting			PartyGaming, Betfair
	Dating			Match.com
	Recruitment			Monster
	C2C market			eBay
	B2B market/exchange			China's e-hub
	Socializing			MySpace, Facebook
Content	Search			Google
	Newspaper, magazine		Wall Street Journal	Blogs
	Music			iTunes
	Film, television			BBC iPlayer
Retail	Services	Travel	easyJet, JetBlue	Expedia
		Financial	First Direct, Schwab	Lending Tree
	Products	Computing, electronics	Dell	Dabs
		Grocery/ general	Tesco, Wal-Mart	Amazon
		Clothing	Gap, Next	ASOS

huge switch into a mainly internet-based distribution model: low-cost airlines, non-branch-based financial services, Dell's direct sales. And there are new e-business retailers founded on an internet model, like Amazon or Expedia, which now dominates the travel agency market in North America.

In all these cases the opportunities created by the internet for radical cost reengineering, as well as for completely reshaping the customer experience, were central to disruption and success.

The above list is the big e-business names, but the internet cost revolution is also being driven in small markets by niche competitors. Take vacation villa rentals. Before the internet, individual property owners mainly reached customers via marketing companies like Spanish Luxury Villas or English Country Cottages. These companies prepared the property content (text and photos), packaged the properties into glossy mail-out brochures, advertised in the travel classifieds, handled availability, inquiries and bookings (mainly by phone and mail) and processed payments. This was an expensive service that typically cost owners 25–35% of gross rental income.

The internet has driven that cost down to less than 5% of gross, or a fixed fee of a few hundred euros per season. Under this model new online marketing sites (like villarenters.com or owners-abroad.com) offer owners a content template and a simple auto-mated bookings engine, attracting visitors via search and keyword management. Owners drop their own text and photos into the template and maintain accurate availability and pricing (at their discretion). Payment and service interaction are via webforms, email and credit card. No more brochures, call centers, print advertising. Customers get a much better service: easier search and online availability. Owners get a higher net yield and can flex pricing more precisely to match demand. The days of the glossy-brochure villa-marketing company are numbered.

Globalization

The second key strategic theme for cost management is globalization. The world is getting very small. Trade barriers, transport costs, connectivity costs, the time it takes to ship or communicate round the world – these have all come down dramatically. You can now think globally about where to make things or where to provide services and carry out internal processes, pursuing the most cost-efficient location.

The globalization trend has worked its way from commodities through manufacturing to services. Commodity traders have brought us goods and culture from all over the world since the Middle Ages, but from the later waves of globalization two countries are now synonymous with the opportunity (or threat, depending on your point of view): China for manufacturing and India for services.

CHINA

In the nineteenth century Great Britain was known as the "work-shop of the world". In the twenty-first century that title belongs to China.

The statistics on the country's manufacturing output are stagger-ing, even if frequent retelling has dulled their impact. Today China produces:

○ 75% of the world's toys
○ 60% of its clothes
○ 50% of its stereos and televisions and VCRs and DVDs
○ 40% of its mobile phones
○ 75% of the US's supply of nutrition and health supplements

The list goes on and on. The Chinese economy has grown at 8–10% a year for the last 15 years, ever since Deng Xiaoping went for a stroll around Shenzhen's factories and pronounced "development is the hard truth". Industrial production and manufacturing exports have grown at 15–20%. China is consuming 30% of the world's steel and 50% of its cement production, as it builds out the infrastructure to support its boom.

China has a population of 1.3 billion people: 10 times that of Japan and 12 times the combined population of the five Asian Tigers, Singapore, Hong Kong, Malaysia, Taiwan and South Korea. King Kong towering over the big cats. For any manufacturing business China is the big story and will be for decades.

Manufacturers in the West are asking themselves: Am I sourcing as much as I can from China? Am I sourcing effectively? Should I be setting up my own plants there? Will I be able to compete with Chinese producers if they come after my end-user markets?

Manufacturers in middle-income economies are scared stiff. What will China do to the Mexican *maquiladora* factories supplying the US, or Poland's plants supplying Germany, or Malaysia's off-shoring business with Japan? China's average manufacturing wage is around 15% of that in Mexico and 5% of that in the US or the UK. And China has an enormous pool of labor that can be shifted from agriculture to industry over the next 20 years – over 300 million people are still working on the land, at $30 a month not $30 an hour.

Even though China has been so successful across so many product categories, there are still areas of huge untapped opportunity. Take automotive parts. A recent McKinsey paper estimated that if Ford and GM were to source 50% of their basic parts from China they would save $10 billion, 25% of their global parts bill.

For the buying departments of western retailers and wholesalers China is an opportunity to cut consumer prices and grow volume. Wal-Mart buys over $10bn from China each year. Shopping in IKEA it seems as if everything you might ever need for the home is only produced in China. A toaster can be cheaper than a loaf of bread.

In fact, the big shock you get these days is the price of something when it's not manufactured in China. Take bathroom fittings, like taps and shower attachments. Many of these are still manufactured in the West, in particular in Germany, at low volumes using very high-cost labor. A lump of cast metal with a smudge of design value, like a basic set of taps, can cost several hundred dollars. The Chinese could make you a supercomputer for that. The key profit-improvement strategy for top European bathroom brand Grohe, when it was taken over by two private equity companies, was to move production to China.

Ignore China at your peril. Retailer Marks & Spencer carried on sourcing most of its clothing from UK suppliers for way too long. This strategy worked in the 1970s and 1980s when its high line volumes and close supply chain management kept the costs and ranges competitive. But by the 1990s it was simply losing the price-point battle with retailers sourcing from Asia. Finally it switched, but with a big loss of market position that it is still struggling to reverse.

As a contrasting success story take Dyson, the UK-based vacuum cleaner business ("no loss of suction") that went from zero to a 20% market share in the US in three years. For many years Dyson seemed like the kind of manufacturing winner that could stay producing in the UK: its success was based on technical innovation and design, its price points were proudly high, and it manufactured in a picturesque West Country setting of rolling fields and Cotswold villages. Then out of the blue, Dyson closed its Wiltshire factory and moved all production to Asia. The Asian factory tripled production in three years, at a 50% cost saving versus the UK, with a better local network of component suppliers. (The company's UK staff numbers did continue to grow, but in R&D, design and marketing.)

INDIA

Manufacturing globalization passed India by. While the Asian Tigers and China mopped up global demand for low-cost televisions, India was stuck in a time warp. Terrible roads, ports and airports. Unreliable power and water. Foreign investment frowned on. Protected local industrial "champions" who couldn't sell outside India. Awful bureaucracy. Stuck at what Indians called the "Hindu growth rate", 4% a year versus China's 8–10%.

Then technology came to the rescue. First off, western companies needed thousands of IT programmers, for Y2K projects, for supporting enterprise systems like SAP and Oracle, for putting businesses online, for the explosion in IT outsourcing. The US produces under 50,000 engineering and IT graduates a year. India produces over 300,000. Indian engineers and engineering schools are world class.

Then there was a revolution in communication and remote working. The internet arrived. Telecoms cost collapsed. Now you could have a remote programming team in India working in parallel with a team in Seattle and they could share work-in-progress in real time at no extra connectivity cost – almost no different from having a second team working down the road in Portland. In India you could create a cocoon of western-style efficiency insulated from the physical chaos outside – satellite connections, private generators, immaculate cubicles, landscaped campuses.

This new remote working wasn't just applicable to IT. Many other activities could now shift to India: contact centers, accounting, claims, records, transcription. This has become India's huge new business process outsourcing industry. BPO provides jobs for millions of Indians, dwarfing the workforce impact of IT and software.

India had one other critical card to play: English. It has the only large-scale pool of low-cost skilled labor that has English as a first-equal language. Out of a total population of 1.2 billion there is an educated middle class of 50 million who are first-language fluent and another 50–100 million who are (or could quickly become) competent to work in English. While there are other pockets of labor capacity like this elsewhere in the world – the Philippines and South Africa – they are not on the scale of India. And nowhere else can you get the combination of large English-speaking capacity plus a significant engineering skills base at low cost.

One liability went away, or at least got smaller. The Indian government stopped blocking foreign investment, cut taxes on computer imports, freed prices on telecoms and started to make the country an attractive and safe place to invest. (Ironically, that is least true of the IT hub, Bangalore, which has awful corruption and infrastructure – India's Garden City is now a Traffic Hell.)

Right now if you're not thinking about how to use India, you're probably slipping behind your competition. Not thinking about India today is like being Sony in the mid-1980s and not thinking about moving manufacturing from Japan to Malaysia. India will do for services businesses and activities what the Tigers and China did for manufacturing, so you need to be pushing the India opportunity across your business as far and as fast as possible.

These days there are many solid offshore vendors to provide competitive tenders, or intermediaries and advisers if you want to set up in-house operations in India. In addition to the well-established locations like Bangalore, Delhi and Mumbai, next-wave places with lower wage rates are growing rapidly, like Chennai, Hyderabad and Puna.

You make savings mainly in direct labor cost – salary plus benefits and payroll taxes. In an Indian software company I work with the direct cost of a programmer is $15,000, versus $90,000 when the same company places an employee onsite with a client in the US. A call center telemarketer or technical support person might cost $4,000 in India versus $20–30,000 in the UK.

Indirect cost, on the other hand, is not much lower than in the West. PCs, software, headsets and telecoms gear are priced globally and in India can actually be more expensive than in Seattle. Facilities up to western standards cost the same as in the West, including back-up generators to cope with power cuts. The ratios of supervisors and trainers can be higher and Indian pay rates for experienced managers are moving up to international levels. You also need to build in extra costs for remote communication and management, and for travel.

The real cost comparison might show India saving you 50–70% vs the US or UK cost. That's a big saving. If your company sells call center services you couldn't compete against that kind of cost advantage.

Having such a low cost base lets you offer extra services that you couldn't do if you were operating from elsewhere. For example, many IT and software companies now offer a Live Chat button in the sales area of their website. Click the button and you are instantly messaging one-to-one with a technical salesperson in India, at any time of the day or night. Your midnight is their midday and vice versa; 24-hour call centers have turned Bangalore into a 24-hour commuter city, packed minibuses racing through the streets at 3 a.m.

With its global service assets the country can move into new off-shore markets. Take healthcare. India has a huge pool of skilled surgeons, doctors and carers. A heart bypass operation there costs £5,000 including airfare and recuperation, versus £15,000 for private treatment in the UK or US.

India's private hospitals have lower death and infection rates than most "developed" countries. Coming from the UK you can sidestep NHS waiting times. And you can recuperate for three weeks under the palm trees on an Indian Ocean white sand beach.

Offshoring is good for the West and very good for India, which previously seemed condemned to slow growth for ever, leaving hundreds of millions in poverty. With offshoring, growth is up to Chinese levels and hundreds of thousands are escaping poverty.

GLOBALIZATION AS A STRATEGIC COST-REDUCTION DRIVE

Just like the internet, globalization offers the opportunity to reduce cost in most functional areas. To maintain a high-level focus you may need a special taskforce, reporting to top management, leading the push.

For manufacturing businesses and production functions, playing the China card is so central these days that this proposal may be redundant. But for service businesses, service functions and back-office processes, India is still a new option. Even the most adventurous have only scraped the surface of the opportunity. A systematic high-level focus will pay dividends.

You can assess the India opportunity line by line on the P&L: purchasing, sales and marketing, R&D, customer service, back-office processing, finance, HR. You can be creative in slicing and dicing to see if some pieces of an activity can be offshored while others stay on shore.

This can throw up unlikely opportunities. A US-based temporary staffing business found that it could do candidate identification,

COST MANAGERS: INFOSYS

Infosys is a great Indian success story, one of the top three leading Indian IT vendors and probably the best-known Indian IT brand. Revenue in 2007–08 was around $4 billion, growing at 35–40% a year. The company was adding over 2,000 new hires a month. The business was valued at over $30 billion, eight times sales, an amazing ratio for an outsourcing business.

The finance department had 40 staff worldwide, one finance person for every 1,000 employees. Even though it had 25% net margins and was doubling revenue every two years, this company was serious about cost management.

Corporate stories mythologized the tough-on-cost mentality. A very large US client came out to Bangalore for some meetings. The Infosys account manager asked the Americans out for dinner and invited a couple of his colleagues, including the then CFO. Dinner was at the Taj, a good but over-the-top and very overpriced hotel for foreigners on expense accounts. The two US clients got there before any of their hosts, so they settled in and ordered a decent bottle of French wine – in India a mortgage-generating decision. The Infosys guys arrived, went a bit pale and next time round ordered some good old Grover local red. When the bill came there was a mass exodus for the bathrooms, leaving the CFO to sign with a shaking hand. The next day a memo went out to the global salesforce: never let the client get to the restaurant first!

Even in India you still have to be tough on cost. You need to reverse some management reflexes picked up in the West, where labor is expensive and capital is cheap; in India the opposite is true. And for some skills, like top-end developers and program managers, labor costs are rising at frantic rates – so you can't just ride a wave of low-cost labor, you have to be smart about structuring compensation and locking in talent.

initial contact, phone interview and reference checking all from India – cutting cost and improving the level and quality of candidate screening before submission to the client. A software business established that it could author and produce most of its sales and marketing collateral in India and run its extranet and intranet there. A television production company discovered that India can deliver high-quality CGI and animation.

You don't have to leap into India in a big way. You can approach it in careful steps: small-scale pilots, running parallel operations for some months, sending key home-based staff to India for one or two years to help manage the transition.

But you do have to make the move – you can be certain your competitors will.

Toolkit – Wired and Global

THE INTERNET

○ Pursue the cost-reduction opportunities offered by the internet creatively and relentlessly.

○ Get all line managers thinking about how the internet could change the heavy costs of interaction with:
  * Suppliers
  * Employees
  * Current customers
  * Potential customers
  * Others (shareholders, analysts, voters)

GLOBALIZATION

○ Pursue the cost-reduction opportunities offered by globalization of production – the China card.

○ And for the globalization of IT and services – the India card:
  * IT
  * Back office
  * Customer service
  * Sales and marketing
  * R&D

8 Lateral Thinking

Though we cannot make our sun
Stand still, yet we will make him run

—Andrew Marvell

So far I've looked at the more straightforward ways of getting a grip on cost: keeping headcount tight, getting tough with suppliers, using the internet, globalization. In this chapter I turn some conventional thinking about cost on its head. I look at the sneakier ways costs get created and the more creative ways they can be cut. When costs get cunning, you need to get smart.

Excess cost can be created by indirect factors that aren't immediately apparent. You can only attack these costs by getting to the real heart of the problem, rather than just bashing away at the cost itself. The three biggest indirect cost generators are time, complexity and poor quality.

I also consider clever ways you can turn cost on its head, get rid of it altogether or turn it into a new profit stream. There may be activities in your business costing you a lot of money that you could get your customers to do for you, for free. They might even prefer that. And there may be some cost lines on your P&L that you can actually turn into revenue. That's the best possible outcome: cost into revenue, water into wine.

Indirect Cost Generators

TIME IS MONEY

Doing things faster reduces cost.

For instance, a big cost in fashion retailing is the markdown or writeoff of stock that hasn't sold. This can be up to 30% of full price across a season's range. Time is the key. The shorter you make the order-to-delivery-to-sale cycle, the lower the risk of getting stuck with stock you can't sell. You can shorten the cycle by:

○ Knowing immediately what's selling in the stores.
○ Using that information to place reorders with your suppliers, quickly and frequently, in small batches.
○ Minimizing shipment time from supplier to store (from China to the Mall of America or to Meadowhall).
○ Being able to reprice quickly at point of sale.

If you shorten this cycle you can reduce other costs as well as write-downs, like warehousing (although you may see some cost lines increase: shipping by air rather than by sea, or shifting reorder production from China to Portugal or Mexico).

As another example take the product development cycle in software. Software developers always want as much time as possible to build product. More time reduces their stress and lets them get closer to the perfect code. However, more time adds much more cost – not just the cost of developer time, but also the risk that the product will be less relevant to its market by the time it finally arrives. 80% of the value of the software end product will have been produced in the first 20% of time and effort. It will be better to get the product released faster and then fix customer issues and bugs in a quick-fire V1.1. If you can reduce cycle time you will dramatically reduce overall cost.

In fact, shortening the cycle is the only real way to get more cost efficient in product development. And it is critical not just, or not even mainly, for cost reasons. If you lose time versus your competitors you lose the market opportunity.

Overall product cycles for items like the iPod or the Wii have come down from several years in the 1970s to a year or less today – and that's the whole product cycle, from idea development through production to sales boom and sales decline.

In 1980 the standard development cycle for a new car, from concept to launch, was four to five years. When Ross Perot joined the GM board around that time, he said that launching a new car took longer than it took America to win the Second World War after being attacked at Pearl Harbor. Now the vehicle development cycle is around a year.

You can apply this short-cycle approach to almost anything:

○ **Annual budgets** – they take too long and take up too much valuable manager time. Start them later, finish them faster, don't put in so many loops and layers.

○ **Meetings** – most are badly organized and last too long. They happen too often; too many people get invited; they could be done by phone. Some companies (like Asda/Wal-Mart in the UK) make everybody stand up throughout meetings, which suddenly become very efficient.

○ **IT deployments** – don't believe the software suppliers when they tell you it takes 18 months to deploy SAP or Siebel. That is going to cost you serious money. Deploy in three months, then pull the plug on external support and let the users fend for themselves. John Reid converted Citibank from paper to computer records as long ago as the 1970s. He had been told it would take years. He went into head office with his wrecking team one weekend and physically threw out all the paper files. Mayhem for a month, then everything worked. As a contrasting example, the

UK government announced in 2000 that it had a 15-year plan for making the country a leader in internet and e-stuff. What can you say to that – a 15-year timeframe in the same sentence as the internet?

O **Consulting projects** – you can get a strategy review done in six months or six weeks. The consultants will want six months for the same reasons as software developers want years to write code. Six weeks will be better for you.

Obviously there can be situations where going faster isn't right, where more haste really is less speed. But these are in the minority. In general, taking time out of processes and decisions squeezes out cost – and it makes you more competitive in what you offer your customers.

COMPLEXITY IS EXPENSIVE

All other things being equal, making things simple and doing them simply will keep costs down.

Take Wanxiang. It is now China's largest auto parts supplier and the third largest private Chinese business. It started in 1969 with $500 in capital as a repair shop for bicycles and tractors. In the way of emerging Asian-economy businesses, it then went through a phase of high-energy but haphazard growth, diversifying into hundreds of products and business lines. In the early 1980s management did an about-turn: out of those hundreds of product lines they sold or closed all except one, universal joints for vehicles. This was a perceptive and radical move for a company at that early stage of evolution. The result? Wanxiang now dominates its target market, supplying the top western automakers, and earns 10% on almost $2 billion of sales.

Wanxiang's management had realized that complexity and lack of focus are the enemy of cost efficiency. Too many product lines mean too little attention available for each, subscale production volumes, slow accumulation of learning.

You start to see a tangible extra cost layer being created in over-complex businesses, a cost layer whose sole *raison d'être* is to analyze and manage the complexity. This might include the highly paid members of a portfolio strategy group spending their time working out which product lines could get pooled into which SBUs. Or top management at diversified media and technology groups like AOL/Time Warner or Sony trying to squeeze convergence and synergy out of fairly unrelated businesses. Or endless pricing and customer profitability analyses from teams of MBAs because you've fallen into the trap of negotiating individual deals with every major customer.

In each case extra complexity has produced extra cost and reduced focus, but it hasn't added any value to your customers or to your business.

Tax is a good example of useless and massively inefficient complexity. Taxes and tax exemptions or allowances build up over time like barnacles. Eventually the cost of administering them (calculating, collecting, exempting, refunding, penalizing) can become the biggest line item of government expenditure. In the US this cost is around 15% of revenue collected. Flat-tax revolutionaries would like to kill this cost of complexity.

Cost-reduction consulting projects can themselves be interesting examples of the cost of complexity. Consultants like selling cross-functional projects. In their pitch they observe that you are organized around functional departments like sales, production, service, distribution and so on. But what really matters, they point out, are key activities that cross functional boundaries, like fulfilling a purchase, or making a customer happy, or delivering quality at Six Sigma levels. These are what really drive cost. This pitch is similar to the reengineering fad of the early 1990s.

If you buy into this, soon you'll be stuck in a hell of cross-functional brainstorming meetings. Your key staff will be tied up for days reinventing the blindingly obvious on process flow diagrams stuck on brown-papered meeting-room walls. At the end of this process you'll get an interesting analysis saying things like: Did you know it costs you $900 to make a customer happy? And not being a quality organization costs you 20% of revenue?

Consultants like these projects because they take ages to do. The conclusions are hard to disprove one way or the other. And the "So what and what do I do about it?" is usually completely opaque, so there's more work to be done.

One European technology company was persuaded to structure a cost-reduction consulting project around its development cycle cost. Cue endless brown-papering sessions as activities and costs were pulled together from marketing, development, operations, customer support, SG&A. Total development cycle costs were finally estimated at €200m ($300m), and the team had found clever cross-functional ways to get that down by €40m ($60m).

Nevertheless, there were two major core problems. Every initiative had at least two line managers' names tagged against it. And it proved impossibly complex (naturally!) to budget and track the savings across multiple line functions. Net net: nobody drove the action program and no costs were cut.

Cross-functional approaches are conceptually appealing. But they break two of the basic rules of good cost management: establish clear individual accountabilities, and avoid complexity.

QUALITY CUTS COST

Back when I was young and easy under the apple boughs, it was thought that you had to choose between cost and quality (or "differentiation" as Porter called it). As I discussed in Chapter 1, you supposedly couldn't be higher quality *and* lower cost.

Japanese manufacturers in the 1970s and 1980s overturned this point of view. Inspired by Deming, an American consultant, they focused on driving up quality, on reducing defects from one in a hundred to one in a million. This gave their cars and televisions an awesome reputation for reliability, much better than GM or Philips.

It became apparent that the Japanese were not having to increase spending to get higher quality. The opposite was true. The more they focused on quality, the more efficient and lower cost they became. This unexpected virtuous cycle became known as the Toyota paradox. It works in several ways.

Eliminating defects before they occur eliminates remedial costs later in the value chain. These remedial costs could be in the factory as goods are checked before being shipped out. Or, more expensively, they could be after goods have reached the end consumer: high warranty claims, product recalls, lawsuits.

Building quality in at the front end also eliminates the need for large quality-control departments at the back end, with their overheads and bureaucracy.

Adopting a zero-tolerance approach to defects tends to squeeze slack out of a system. Take just-in-time (JIT) inventory, a technique also pioneered by Toyota. Before JIT, manufacturers used to build up buffer stocks at several stages of the production process, to provide a cushion in case of a supply breakdown. The Japanese discovered that those buffer stocks actually reinforced the problems they were meant to solve: because they existed, managers got sloppy, tolerating stoppages, delivery failures, bad scheduling. And of course holding the buffer stocks was itself a big cost.

Under JIT all buffer stocks were eliminated. When that slack was taken out of the system, not only were inventory costs cut back but overall production efficiency improved, as there was no longer anywhere to hide. A higher-quality process produced a lower-cost process.

Let the Customers Do the Work

I grew up next to a pre-self-service Sainsbury's grocery store in South London. You queued, ordered and paid at different counters for meat and fish, dairy, jars of jam and cans of vegetables. It was a rather beautiful experience, particularly the slicing and wrapping of butter on marble slabs and the sawdust on the tiled floor. But heavens, it took a long time. And there was a lot of labor involved in all that good old-fashioned service.

My parents switched overnight when given the choice of self-service. You halved your shopping time. Prices were much lower. As the stores got bigger you got more choice and you could buy most things in one visit. This was a win–win for retailers and consumers. Everybody cut cost and saved time. These days we've gone even further: we can price-scan our own baskets and with RFID tags we should soon be able to walk straight out of the store without any human contact. (Although there are still some strange hangovers from the 1950s, like checkout baggers in the US. Is this a covert federal job-creation scheme?)

You can get your customers to put in extra time and extra work, to do the work for you, if they can get a better price. IKEA can get me to scrabble around on the floor for hours in a demented haze of screwdrivers and assembly instructions, just to save $10 on a kitchen table. Even the first time I did that, years ago when I was a junior whipper-snapper consultant, my billing rate was $100 an hour, but there I'd be, saving $5 an hour fighting with flatpacks. And I'd be back next week to buy the matching kitchen dresser. Those cunning Swedes had tapped into the fact that I valued my time when I was shopping at close to zero. They could unload a pile of cost onto me and I'd love them for giving me a bargain.

On the internet I'm happy to do myself all the stuff that a travel agent or an airline used to do for me and charge me for: research, book, ticket, change, cancel. And I am faster than most agents, I can find the best deal and I can do it at midnight when my time cost really is zero – and on top of all that I actually *like* doing it (sad but true).

Or I can use the internet to do technical self-help to fix a PC problem. Fifteen minutes searching an online help database is a lot better than an hour on hold with the "customer service" phone line.

If you can, get customers to do the work. If it speeds things up for them, or if they do it better than your staff would, they'll prefer it – and the cost is off your P&L.

Cost into Revenue

The best thing to do with cost is to turn it into revenue. You might be able to do this partially, getting in some offsetting revenue; or totally, turning a cost center into a profit opportunity.

MENU PRICING

Changing pricing can help cut costs. To see how, you need to visualize a spectrum of possible pricing strategies. At one end is bundled pricing, or "solutions selling", where a customer is given a total price comprising many elements. At the other end is unbundled or menu pricing, where customers get to see the price of individual components and cherry-pick the bits they want.

Bundled solutions help customers when what they are buying is complex and risky, or in an early stage of development and so not yet understood. This is how Cisco sells communications infrastructure, or Siebel and Accenture sell CRM implementations. This was how AOL bundled ISP, email and portal for confused non-techies in the early days of the internet. Customers were more concerned about ease of use and reliability than about cost.

As markets mature, customers understand better what they are buying and will take on more risk. At that stage menu pricing can help both sellers and buyers reduce cost.

As an example take the GDS business, the travel reservation systems that link airlines and travel agents, which I discussed in Chapter 5. After the agencies had the option of switching to standard PCs, the internet and e-ticketing, the technology was cheaper, easier to use and more reliable. But since everything was still bundled into one packaged price, agencies had no incentive to work with the GDSs on reducing overall system cost, so cost wasn't coming down as fast as it should have been. The answer was to move to menu pricing. Basic access cost was cut dramatically. Then agents were given a menu of optional services with additional costs. They could still get PCs supplied and maintained by the GDS or they could buy them themselves. They could continue to get help desk support from the GDS, but now they would be charged per minute or per response so their call frequency dropped significantly. This change stimulated win–win behaviour.

The airline industry itself has moved to menu pricing – in good and bad ways.

On the good side, the airlines have unbundled the costs associated with sales channel, service, payment and airport choice. Take a trip I'm making from London to Toulouse. My two cost options, on the same airline, could look like those opposite. Choosing the high-cost menu options could more than double the cost of my trip. But the airline and I are set up to achieve a win–win. If I eliminate their costs of agency commissions, credit card fees, paper tickets and call centers, I get the cost benefits. I can choose which airport to travel from and pay different airport charges, as well as deciding how much luggage to take. In the future I might choose to pay for manual check-in.

On the bad side this can be taken to extremes, with extra charges for security, airport and air travel taxes or fuel. Or consider a "free"

	HIGH-COST OPTIONS	££	LOW-COST OPTIONS	££
Basic flight cost		70		70
Menu of extra charges				
Sales (booking)	Travel agent	20	Direct online	0
Payment	Credit card	5	Electron card	0
Ticket	Paper	25	eTicket	0
Check-in	Manual	5	Electronic	0
Baggage	Max in the hold	30	Small hand only	0
Subsequent name change	Phone	50	Internet	25
Airport charges	Heathrow/TLS	25	Gatwick/TLS	15
Menu extras total		160		40
TOTAL COST		230		110

Airmiles flight, which can end up more expensive than a fully inclusive booking on a low-cost carrier.

Car rental companies can exploit menu pricing as well. I booked a car at Madrid airport at a great pre-paid rate, $35 a day. I'd checked that the rate included all the usual suspects: mileage, insurance, local taxes etc. But my final bill was $70 a day. That creative rental company had come up with airport supplements, franchise fees (franchise fees?), exchange rate charges, insurance against excess charges on the normal insurance, and on and on.

My favorite menu-pricing scam was a billing change by a UK cable company renowned for having the worst customer service on the planet. Every month I got a bill for £24.99. Then one month it went up to £25.99. The new bill looked like this:

MR WILEMAN'S CABLE ACCOUNT	
Cable service	24.99
Charge for itemized billing	1.00
TOTAL	25.99

TURN COST CENTERS INTO PROFIT CENTERS

Sometimes you can turn costs into full-blown profit centers.

Take Carnival Cruise Lines, the world's largest cruise business. Its awesome 3,000-passenger ships tower over the Miami docks as you drive by with the roof down on the causeway from Downtown to South Beach. One of the company's biggest costs used to be the cleaning and maintenance of cabins. No longer. Now self-employed husband-and-wife teams bid to get the "franchise" to clean and maintain a package of 20 or 30 cabins. The tips they get (that customers are rather strongly encouraged to give) can make this a highly profitable small business. They are motivated to give very good service. And Carnival has turned a big cost line into a profit center.

Or take technical publishing, such as scientific or management journals. Many years ago you had to pay scientists to write the content. Then in the 1950s Robert Maxwell, running the Pergamon business that made his fortune, found that actually scientists would give you content for free. They needed to publish to build their academic reputation and to meet publication targets in order to keep their university jobs.

Similarly, management academics and management consultants need to market themselves and their ideas in management and trade journals to reach potential executive clients. They will also give you high-quality content free. They will even do proprietary research for the journals if they get sponsor recognition. Crossing over to the Dark Side, the less ethical may even quietly buy up thousands of copies of their own business books to make them into bestsellers. (I have myself put in a small advance order for 10,000 copies of this book.)

So professional publishing can come pretty close to the ideal business: customers pay you to read the stuff and writers pay you to let them write it.

You can use this idea in situations where there is heavy customer demand for an underresourced service. For example, an enterprise software company had to cope with a deluge of requests from its installed customer base for upgrades and custom features. The company was continually expanding its expensive professional services team, whose time was not charged to customers, but was failing to keep up with customer demand. Costs were ballooning. Customers were very unhappy. Deciding which of them would get serviced first was a pretty random process.

The problem was solved by charging for professional services and by auctioning their time to the highest bidder. The company was worried that doing this would alienate their customers. The opposite ended up being true. Customers felt in control of their fate again. If their problem was really material and urgent, they didn't mind paying to get a rapid response. Introducing a market mechanism turned cost into revenue and produced happier customers.

Toolkit – Lateral Thinking

TIME IS MONEY
○ Are all your business processes as fast as possible?
○ Where could you reduce cycle time and save cost?

COMPLEXITY IS EXPENSIVE
○ Can you cut costs by simplifying what you do and how you do it?
○ If the complexity is deliberate, are you sure its value exceeds its cost?
○ Can you get most of the value but with less cost?

QUALITY CUTS COST
○ Could you invest more up front in quality to get an overall reduction in cost?
○ Could you reduce back-end costs like quality control, rework, service recovery, product recalls?

LET THE CUSTOMERS DO THE WORK

○ Are there activities you do, and pick up the costs for, that your customers could do better and more cheaply?

○ Would customers actually prefer to do some things for themselves?

TURN COST INTO REVENUE

○ Are there some cost lines that you could turn into revenue?

○ Could menu pricing lower net costs for you and for your customers?

○ Could you get for free things you now pay for, or even better get people to pay you?

○ Could some of your cost centers become profitable third-party businesses?

Cost Management as Strategy

Being a good cost manager, with a deep understanding of cost dynamics, is far more than just a tactical operational asset. It can provide the basis for strategic competitive advantage by enabling you to:

○ Deliver value through acquisitions.
○ Price strategically.
○ Discover more new growth opportunities.
○ Preserve value creation in large corporations with multiple business units.

Delivering Value via Acquisitions

Most acquisitions don't create value for the acquiring company's shareholders. Despite this well-known and well-researched fact, companies remain dead keen on acquisitions and investment bankers continue to make their millions by feeding that enthusiasm.

Most acquisitions don't create value because the price paid for the acquired company is typically 30–50% higher than the price was before the acquisition process started. This is the "acquisition premium". So acquisition strategies need to set out what extra synergies will be created in the new, combined larger business to earn out that premium.

There are two main types of synergy: "scope" and "scale". Scope synergy generally involves generating more revenue. Scale synergy involves lowering unit cost.

A good example of a merger based on scope or revenue synergy was Time Warner and AOL. This was a classic new/old-media combo. The idea was to put Time Warner's stable of old-media brands and content out through AOL's internet brand and channel, and to use AOL's tech savvy to add other new-media channels, in both cases generating more revenue for both sides.

Or take mobile phones. A mobile operator in France buys an operator in Germany partly because it thinks it will get more overall business from customers (particularly business customers) in both countries if they can seamlessly roam in France and Germany while staying on its network. It might stretch the logic to buying an operator in India, not so much to get more revenue from the same customer but because the company thinks it knows ways of getting more revenue faster from the Indian business, from its experience in other countries.

There are countless examples of acquisition-led strategies based on synergies of scope or revenue. Retail banks buying insurance brands to sell through their branches, or wholesale banks venturing into the dangerous waters of investment banking. Or travel conglomerates, like Cendant, trying to bundle up hotels, cars, time-shares, travel agencies, booking systems, package tours. And there may be several *successful* examples. However, the probability of failure is higher than with cost-based strategies (or with strategies based on revenue and cost).

The examples above are reasonably representative. The Time Warner/AOL combination was a disaster for Time Warner's shareholders and promised synergies around revenue, content and technology barely materialized. Cendant was another financial disaster (actually the travel industry has a history littered with bad conglomerates) and has now been unwound into its component parts.

Investment professionals estimate that mobile operators have blown hundreds of billions of dollars of shareholder value in their race for global presence – Vodafone alone may be in the $100bn blown-it range. In financial services investors have generally made better returns from conservative firms that stayed narrow in focus and acquired mainly to obtain cost synergies.

The failure rate is higher with revenue synergies because the target benefits could be achieved by ways other than acquisition – ways that are less risky and much easier to execute. A retail bank does not need to acquire an insurance business, it can simply distribute insurance product for a margin. French and German mobile operators can agree to cooperate on roaming to deliver a seamless customer service and simply share the extra revenue gains (this is now what most operators do). Time Warner could have done an arm's-length content deal with AOL and could have acquired Internet savvy by paying out mega-bucks sign-on bonuses to a few hot-shot techies, saving itself around $50bn.

Deals based on scale or cost synergy have a higher chance of success. They are easier to understand and model, easier to execute and the outcome is more reliable.

For example, take the building materials trade distribution sector, what are known in the UK as builders' merchants. The three UK leaders are Wolseley, St Gobain (trading as Jewsons) and Travis Perkins. The sector has been steadily rolled up over the last 20 years, changing from being very fragmented to a situation where the top three represent over 50% of the general merchant market. The roll-up has been done mainly by acquisition, with the main players buying up local and regional competitors. Value creation in this acquisition process has come mainly from cost saving.

You can see how the numbers work in the simplified model overleaf (I've disguised the absolute numbers). The smaller acquired company starts off at 10% of the size of the big three acquirer. It has to hold similar price levels to stay competitive. But it is buying on

Builders merchants acquisition, illustrative

	Big 3 acquirer	Acquired company Pre-acq	Acquired company Post-acq
Pricing, index	100	100	100
Volume, index	100	10	10
% to sales			
Cost of goods, after all			
rebates	-65	-69	-65
Branch cost	-20	-20	-20
Central cost	-7	-7	-5
Operating profit	8	4	10

much worse terms because of its smaller scale, at a disadvantage of maybe 4% of sales (6–7% of buying price). Other cost ratios are similar to the big three player. The smaller company is still privately owned so its owner-manager is quite happy to survive on half the operating profitability that the big three firm needs as a publicly quoted business.

Post-acquisition, the big three firm puts all the purchases onto its better terms, saving 4% on the acquired sales. It also knocks out at least half of the central SG&A costs (like accounting, credit control, IT, buying team), folding the smaller operation easily into its existing head office infrastructure, saving an extra 3% on sales. It probably can't get much out of the branch costs; these are highly variable, with no big scale effects, and smaller merchants usually run a tight ship.

So post-acquisition the big three player has upped the return on the incremental sales from 4% profitability to 10%: more than its average on existing business. In the process it will have been able to split the gain with the small company owner, so he or she gets a richer buyout price (based on maybe a 6–7% profit margin) and the big three acquirer gets enough extra margin to earn out the acquisition premium.

Being a strong cost manager clearly gives you strategic advantage in these cost-based acquisition opportunities. If you are confident that you can get the synergies and that you can hit the top end of possible cost savings, you will be able to bid in more situations, you should be able to justify higher bids and you should end up winning more deals. If there is a roll-up race you stand a better chance of winning. And leadership in the race is self-reinforcing – the bigger your scale, the more synergies you should be able to extract from the next acquisition.

There is also tremendous cumulative value that comes from doing lots of similar deals, learning what works and what doesn't work and becoming steadily more effective at post-acquisition implementation.

The best acquisition situations are where you get solid, reliable cost synergies and you get good revenue synergies: scale *and* scope. The soft drinks business mentioned overleaf is a good example. Also Cisco: when it was on top form, around the year 2000, it had a nice model for bolting smaller telecoms equipment businesses onto an integrated sales and distribution machine, slashing overhead cost and getting a multiplier on revenue.

Lastly, I need to give special mention, a *légion d'honneur* medal, to those acquisitions that are based on negative cost synergies. The French are masters of this type of acquisition and Air France used to be the best practitioner. Before Europe deregulated its skies, Air France would buy up any regional French airline that dared to operate anything more than a couple of turbo-prop flights, on the grounds that the market needed "order" and stable (i.e. high) prices. One airline it bought was Air Inter. Its first action was to raise the salaries of Air Inter staff up to Air France levels, which were about 25% higher. *La synergie de coûts negatifs à la française.*

COST SYNERGIES IN EXTREMIS

I was once working with a top international soft drinks company. It was acquiring small soft drinks businesses and brands in Europe and rolling them into its much more powerful distribution machine. In the process it also consolidated the acquired businesses' overhead functions, as far as possible, into its single head office. My consulting team was involved in modeling post-deal financials and the supportable acquisition premium.

A key assumption in the model was how much we could save in overhead cost. My client had a general manager troubleshooter, Bert, who got parachuted in for the first six months after a deal to put new structures in place. I remember a working session with Bert about how much overhead cost (finance, HR, marketing, the usual suspects) would remain in the acquired business post-deal. I was thinking maybe 70%, i.e. a 30% cut, which would be a pretty aggressive assumption in most sizeable acquisitions.

Bert said, "Zero."

"Bert, it can't be zero. It's never zero. We can't add half a dozen big brands, hundreds of customers, three factories and not add any central cost. It's an insane assumption."

Bert said, "Zero." He was on a mission to destroy. That overhead was dead meat.

I think in the end we agreed on 50% and Bert delivered it.

Underpinning Pricing Strategies

Good cost management helps you use pricing as a competitive weapon.

PRICE WARS: MARKET LEADERS AND MARKET ATTACKERS

Research in the 1960s and 1970s at General Electric and then at Harvard showed a strong relationship between market leadership and long-run profitability. (This was the PIMS project, now being carried on by the Strategic Planning Institute. PIMS initially stood for Profit Impact of Market Share but has morphed into Profit Impact of Market Strategy.) For example, you might see a market where the number one player makes a 10% return on sales, the number two 6%, the number three 2% and smaller players make losses. This is such a generally observable outcome that one of Jack Welch's core rules at GE was that a business had to be number one or two in its market segment, or have a plan for how to become so, or it would be divested.

Market leaders get higher returns via premium pricing and lower unit costs. Smaller players have to fight harder and smarter to overcome those structural disadvantages.

But market leaders face constant attack from those smaller competitors and from new entrants, who'd like to get a bigger slice of that juicy profit pie. The most common line of attack is a price war. Price wars cannot be avoided. But if attackers see that a leader has structural cost advantage (from scale) and tight operational cost management, and is not complacent and bloated, they will back off faster and profit damage will be minimized. Strong cost management reinforces the returns of market leadership by reducing the probability of a price attack, the duration of an attack and the depth of an attack.

Of course, if you are an attacker the logic also holds for you. If you are very low cost and you are facing a bloated incumbent, you have a shot at disrupting the market with aggressive pricing.

NEW PRODUCT INTRODUCTIONS:
PRICING DOWN THE EXPERIENCE CURVE

If you are confident in your ability to drive down costs, you can price ahead of the game to build leadership in new product categories.

Take an electronics product category like widescreen televisions. These are initially very expensive to produce: technology is uncertain, R&D costs have not been written off, production volumes are low, cumulative production is small. But if you are confident that you can manage costs down over the next two or three years, you can price low, based on an expected future experience curve and future tight cost delivery. You can gain an early lead and convert that into market leadership, which gives you a chance of super-returns when the market matures.

This is a core dynamic in markets like MP3 players, mobile phones, personal computers and televisions. Shortening product lifecycles make the dynamics even more challenging and increase the advantage you can gain from being a top-end cost manager.

LONG-TERM CUSTOMER CONTRACTS:
PROFITABLE COMMITMENTS

More customers are looking to sign longer-term contracts with fewer suppliers, as part of a strategic shift to outsourcing or a concentration on fewer better suppliers. In winning this kind of long-term business, and in making money on it, it helps to be very good at predicting and controlling future costs.

Take airline IT outsourcing. IT is a big cost for traditional full-service airlines, running at up to 3% of revenue. It is also business critical. IT underpins pricing, booking, check-in, aircraft movements. IT failure produces operational chaos and enrages customers – think of the baggage-handling system at Heathrow's infamous Terminal 5. So historically large airlines did most of their IT in-house.

But airlines' IT needs are pretty similar. There should be benefits from subscribing to a shared "community" system, with IT being outsourced by many airlines to a common third-party vendor.

The risks, however, are as large for a vendor as they are for the airline. Developing a community platform is expensive. Getting the first one or two airlines up and running will be loss making. And, most importantly, the airlines will only sign up if they are given a contractual commitment on how their IT costs will develop over 10 years. Otherwise they won't lock themselves in to a third-party vendor on a critical functionality.

If you are an intelligent cost manager you have a better chance of getting this kind of business. And you have a better chance of getting it at the right price – a price that gives the airlines the cost savings they need but you the chance of making a good return, not a black hole of future losses.

Discovering More New Growth Opportunities

Back in the dot-com bubble days of 2000, you could get $5m VC (venture capital) money for just an idea, for a café conversation, a concept on a napkin, a five-minute spreadsheet that showed how you only needed 1% of a global trillion-dollar market to make piles of money. Then once you actually had one or two techies on board, beta software and a couple of trial customers, you could get an extra $50m and hire a national salesforce. There were hundreds of businesses that were given that kind of money. Almost all of them blew the lot. The best dot-com expense extravaganza I knew of was Boo.com, an online fashion start-up, which went through over $100m in not much more than 100 days, most of it spent on team-building champagne dinners and Concorde trips.

These days, in the Web 2.0 era, VCs say: "$500k is the new $5m". No VC will invest $5m in a saloon-bar idea, unless you're Steve

Jobs. They might stump up $500,000 – but actually they'd like to see some functioning software for that and one or two trial customers.

You could interpret this change as VCs getting more risk averse. So many got burned so badly in Web 1.0 that now they're more cautious and skeptical.

There is truth in that interpretation, but it's only half the story. VCs have realized that they were thinking about those early-stage investments the wrong way. Sure, it was a bet on a team and an idea. But it was also a cost of experimentation, a cost to find something out. And as such it was way too high and they aren't going to pay at that level in Web 2.0. Now they are driving down the cost of finding out whether a new business idea has legs or not. They're saying to the entrepreneurs: "Find much lower-cost ways of proving your idea and getting it up and running."

So as an aspiring entrepreneur you've got to be a tight cost manager in the development and experimentation phases of your business idea. You might think this is great for the VC, lowering his or her risk, but only negative for you, making you struggle harder to get the business off the ground. You'd be wrong: it's very good for you too.

It forces you from Day 1 to find new, low-cost ways of developing a product, finding a customer, delivering a service. This can open up whole new business approaches that then become core and give your business a competitive advantage. For example, Google set out very early on to run the lowest-cost server farms on the planet, taking a (what was then very unusual) make-it-in-house proprietary approach, which has stood it in great stead as the business has grown to a huge scale.

If you get (and spend) too much money early on, you don't develop good habits and insights into new business models. You keep thinking, well, I'll throw money at the problem until I build scale, then I'll be OK. Or you just get profligate.

There's an even better reason for you, the entrepreneur, to be as tight as hell in the early discovery stages. The less money you need, the more equity you get to keep. Any equity you sell early on you're going to sell cheap. So don't sell it unless and until you absolutely need to; only sell the minimum you need to; and cut your early-stage costs to the bone.

I had a classic conversation along these lines recently with an aspiring India-based entrepreneur who wanted to set up an offshore remote tutoring service for American students. Not a bad idea actually, and I think some variant on it will take off. But he already wanted way too much money, let's say $1m, as a first-stage investment in the idea. He wanted to hire 20 tutors, develop the tutoring software, set up a sales and marketing organization in the US, pay himself a base salary and lose money for at least a year. But he had not taken a series of much smaller, cheaper steps to advance his knowledge of whether and how this would work. He could have sat in on focus groups with students in the US or watched how they work already with face-to-face tutors. He could have done a trial with one or two tutors for three months with a handful of students. These smaller steps could have been done for maybe $10,000 or $20,000.

I was negative and he got upset. But he was upset for the wrong reason: he thought I had no belief in the opportunity. As I said, I thought it was a reasonable idea, but I didn't know for certain if it was a good idea, or whether he was the man to make it work. So the question for me was: how much should it cost me to find out more? His proposed cost was way too much and badly thought through, which did not increase my confidence in him. Also, if in a moment of madness I were to be convinced to invest $1m, at this stage I'd want some huge percentage of the business, maybe 70%, because he was not yet bringing enough value added to the table. If he were to spend three or six months of his own time, plus $20,000 cash, on the small, cheap discovery steps, then maybe he could come back and ask for $1m, have a better chance of getting it and only have to give up 30% of the equity for it. (You can see this drama played out in *Dragon's Den.*)

The benefits of driving down the costs of discovery, and so open-ing up more growth opportunities, apply equally to large corpora-tions. I recently did a strategy workshop for a large corporate client, looking at how it should be investing discretionary cash across a range of potential options. "Discretionary cash" meant capex over and above that needed to maintain existing operations and facilities, plus to cover operating losses from early-stage businesses. The options we were looking at were accelerated domestic expansion of existing brands, entry into new product categories, entry into new channels or formats, international expansion and commercial prop-erty development.

In theory there need be no constraint on how many of these growth avenues to pursue. If they all showed a strong positive return above the cost of capital, we should be able to raise extra equity or debt to fund all of them. In practice, however, the market will only tolerate a certain level of investment losses set against core cash flow – particularly if they are in organic growth rather than acquisitions. So how many potential growth opportunities we could pursue would depend partly on how efficient we could be at driving down the cost of discovery – risking less money per experiment. The more we could behave like a jealous entrepreneur, hugging cash and equity to our chest, the more chips we could get to play with.

One result from this workshop was particularly encouraging. Although we wanted to push existing brands as fast as possible down the e-commerce channel, we were worried about the fixed costs of setting up a group e-commerce infrastructure. But our head of e-commerce, working with IT, had come up with a fantastically low-cost approach. Capex and operating losses were actually negligible, so we could pull all the stops out. This was a change from e-commerce investment discussions even a few years before, when (like my Indian tutor entrepreneur) there would be demands for huge up-front investment in a perfect fully formed environment, way ahead of revenue.

Creating an Effective Center in a Large Corporation

Almost all large corporations, of Fortune 500 or FTSE 100 size, comprise a collection of business units. One of the biggest challenges and tensions in these large corporations is the role and value (or detraction from value) of the center – the central management team and shared support services.

Let's put ourselves for the moment on the board of such a large corporation. On the one hand we want to maintain full profit-and-loss accountability in our business units (BUs), with the BU manager feeling completely in control of his or her destiny. On the other hand we want to get maximum value from our overall corporate scale, in those shared service functions where scale should matter, where we can get lower operating cost or better buying terms or where cross-BU benefits can justify investment in more expertise. We need to get this balance right. We also need to kill the natural tendency of well-funded central bureaucracies to destroy value: with make-work behavior, empire building, fat-cat salaries and expenses, decision paralysis or second-guessing, excessive internal process, distraction from external markets.

Getting this balance wrong is one of the main hazards of being a large corporation. It is one of the main signs of weakness to potential predators, like private equity or hostile trade buyers. Anti-center jokes ("we're from the center, we're here to help"; "when the company builds a new corporate HQ, sell the stock!") capture a hard reality.

A strong cost-management culture is key to creating an efficient and effective center and so being able to build a great multibusiness corporation. Here are some useful tactics for making sure you get the kind of center you need.

MAKE DECENTRALIZATION THE DEFAULT POSITION

Line accountability must be the primary organizational value. The default position should be to decentralize everything down to the BUs and only bring things into the center by exception, where there is a very powerful case (cost or quality) for a central function. Small cost advantages, more elegance or consistency in functional approaches, less messy operational reviews – these are not good enough reasons to centralize.

This principle applies even to cerebral functions like strategy development. Some large corporations still fall into the trap of thinking of BU management as running day-to-day operations, while out-of-the-box future strategy thinking gets done at the center. Absolutely the reverse should be true. (I am writing this paragraph having just come out of a management conference where we were pushing strategy responsibility down to a group of BU managers who had been passive on that front for some years. They needed some pushing to take up the strategy gauntlet; they had been quite happy mildly complaining about lack of strategic direction.)

ESTABLISH A CLEAR SUPPLIER–CUSTOMER
RELATIONSHIP BETWEEN THE CENTER AND BUSINESS UNITS

Wherever possible, central functions should deal with the BUs as if they were external customers. They should be as responsive and efficient as they would be if they faced the risk of losing that customer, rather than treating it as a captive relationship that comes low on the to-do list.

This does not need any big bureaucratic process, like setting up SLAs (service level agreements); internal SLAs are usually not worth the time or pain. It is mainly about principle, attitude and day-to-day behavior. It can be semi-policed by an annual customer satisfaction survey, conducted by a third party, with high-profile feedback loops and real teeth.

The idea of customer satisfaction feedback is a good reality check on the center's true attitudes. When I raised it recently with one central services director, he said: "OK, that's fine, but I want to be able to rate the BUs as well, on how well they use my wonderful services, because some of the BU managers are useless." That may have been fair comment, but I can't imagine I'd be happy about my mobile operator giving me an annual rating on whether I'm a good customer!

BE PARTICULARLY HARD ON CENTER COST CREEP

You need to be particularly paranoid about central cost creep. It has bad indirect effects on productivity and focus in the BUs. And it sends very bad signals to the whole corporation – including some costs that may be financially trivial but have large symbolic value, like secretarial support or travel and entertainment.

ESTABLISH AND TRACK HARD METRICS ON CENTER EFFICIENCY

This is key to getting a level playing field around performance pressure and performance measurement. The BUs get pushed and tracked objectively around their P&L performance, versus budget and prior year. BU managers get their bonuses or not based on hard targets and hard data. Central function performance, in contrast, is often opaque, leading to suspicion on the part of the BUs that the center is not being driven hard, is ducking and diving around targets, and gets its bonuses regardless.

So you need to find metrics to establish an objective targeting and tracking of center performance: unit cost, productivity, service delivery, customer satisfaction, competitive benchmarking. And you need to make that process fair and visible, creating an equivalent to the

BU budget setting and reporting, with regular monthly and quarterly reviews.

DO ANNUAL PRIVATE EQUITY-TYPE
REVIEWS THAT CHALLENGE THE CENTER

A good discipline in the annual planning process is to get a senior executive to play devil's advocate and challenge the entire central structure and cost, taking a private equity-style stance, arguing for a slash-and-burn attack on central overhead. Then the center managers have to defend their value.

PRIVATE EQUITY SECRETS

John Lovering is one of the UK's most successful managers in private equity. He has been a chairman-investor in nine deals over the last ten years, including Odeon, Homebase, Fitness First, Debenhams and Somerfield.

His three secrets of PE are: "Buy well, sell well, and don't bugger it up too much in the middle."

If there's no difference between good management in private and public companies, how can PE do it better? "Get rid of initiative overload," Lovering urges. "Public companies are run by clever people issuing new ideas every Monday." So get rid of the nice-to-have initiatives. "Weaken the staff departments – make heroes out of the line. If your job is called integrative strategic advisory consultative person, you are out of a job.

"Raise the bar. PE change can be very Maoist. It's a one-off opportunity to set higher expectations." Although he admits it is difficult to stay radical for long: "So we don't allow ourselves to get bored, we make it explicit with our goals and our three to five-year timeframes."

In a PE regime, Lovering says that executives and shareholders have the same goals: "The IT head is no longer interested in doing the best SAP implementation ever so he can put it on his CV, unless it really generates cash."

Toolkit – Cost Management as Strategy

DELIVER VALUE VIA ACQUISITIONS
○ Most acquisitions don't add value, but a strong cost manager has a much better chance of doing so.
○ Cost-based synergies are better than revenue- or scope-based ones.

UNDERPIN PRICING STRATEGIES
○ In price wars – for market leaders and market attackers.
○ In new product introductions – pricing down the experience curve.
○ In long-term customer contracts – making profitable commitments.

DISCOVER MORE NEW GROWTH OPPORTUNITIES
○ Drive down the cost of discovery.
○ Retain more equity value.

CREATE AN EFFECTIVE CENTER IN A LARGE CORPORATION
○ Make decentralization the default position
○ Establish a clear supplier–customer relationship between the center and the business units.
○ Be particularly hard on center cost creep.
○ Establish and track hard metrics around center efficiency.
○ Do annual private equity-type reviews that challenge the center.

Cost in the Public Sector

Great nations are never impoverished by private, although they sometimes are by public prodigality and misconduct. The whole, or almost the whole public revenue, is in most countries employed in maintaining unproductive hands. Such are the people who compose a numerous and splendid court...

—Adam Smith, *The Wealth of Nations*

The public sector presents the biggest cost-management challenge. Getting it right increases living standards and opportunity today. Getting it wrong creates a dead-weight drag on the future. We need to throw down the gauntlet to politicians, civil servants and public-sector managers, and to the voting public, challenging them to champion the drive for efficiency and value.

The ideas described in this book have been developed from working in the private sector and they can usefully be applied to public-sector cost management. But to be open kimono (a visually disturbing business metaphor), I have not personally worked much in the public sector. So in this chapter I am arguing from logic and research, not from the deep first-hand experience of the rest of the book.

The Size of the Problem

Government spending – there certainly is a lot of it. In Western Europe public spending is usually 40–50% of GDP. The French and

Swedes are at 50–60%, the Irish and Swiss at 35%. The UK was a low-end outlier in the late 1990s at 35%, but a recent Labour government public spending bonanza pushed it back up over 40%. This is going against the trend in almost every other OECD country, a theme I'll come back to later.

Outside Europe the numbers are lower. The US and Australia are both around 35%; Canada, Japan and New Zealand are nearer 40%.

35–60% of GDP. These are VERY LARGE numbers.

What is this spending made up of? As an example, in 2005 UK public-sector spending, ignoring interest payments, was around £500bn or $1 trillion. The big components were:

○ "Social protection" (welfare payments, child and pensioner support) – 30%.
○ Health ("free" universal healthcare provision) – 18%.
○ Education (schools and universities) – 14%.
○ Public order and safety (police, courts, firefighting) plus defense – 12%.
○ Social services, transport, industry/agriculture/employment/training, housing and environment – about 4% each.

There are 60 million Brits, so that £500bn is over £8,000 ($16,000) per citizen.

IS THIS A PROBLEM AND WHY?

Right now in the richer Western economies, lower state spending is likely to be a good thing.

Before the First World War, the state in the US and the UK was a minnow compared with what we take for granted today. Taxes and government spending were 10% of GDP.

Then came the 1917 Russian revolution. Soon Russia gave us the other end of the spectrum, the first full Communist state, controlling 90% of GDP. That's the magnitude of the range in the early years of the twentieth century: capitalism at 10% of GDP, communism at 90%.

Over the century the tide of battle ebbed and flowed, from the 1920s Great Depression to the breakup of the Soviet Union. And here's where we've ended up today: bang in the center ground, with the state at 35–60% of GDP. Any red-in-tooth-and-claw American capitalist from the Rockefeller era would be incredulous that in the US the government is now swallowing up 35% of the economy. It's all over, the Commies have won!

A state spend at 35% of GDP can be considered OK, as can funding large amounts of income redistribution and safety nets, universal access to healthcare and education, strong law and order, good local community services. But above 35% people get nervous, and above 40% they get very nervous.

Many advanced economies went through their "what-percentage-should-the-state-be" experiments in the 1980s and 1990s. The vast majority have spent the last decade or two pulling back from levels that had got too high. But quite apart from the issue of the absolute percentage level, I want to get value for money from the amounts that the government is spending on my behalf. I want the state to be a tough cost manager. Is that likely?

Why Managing Public-Sector Cost Is Tough

Managing public-sector cost *is* tough. Why and how, and exactly how tough, depend on which chunk of spending you're talking about.

TRANSFERS AND SUBSIDIES

This covers the 30% spent, in the UK example above, on social protection, welfare benefits for unemployment or disability, support for children or older people, and so on. As a citizen, I can have a view on who should get what, for how long, under what conditions, with what checks and processes. I can have my view on what a fair society should do. Others will have different opinions and we express our views at the ballot box.

Once democratic debate and vote have produced a conclusion, however imperfect, I can put my cost manager's hat back on. I want the public money flows to go effectively to the targets that have been politically agreed, I don't want money to go to the wrong targets, and I want administration of this whole complex activity to cost as little as possible.

For example, in the UK you can get "normal" unemployment benefit or you can get "incapacity" (i.e. disability- or injury-based) benefit. Since the 1980s it has been much more attractive to be classified as being on incapacity: you get more money, it is easier to claim, you get it for longer. So no surprise: the welfare market has responded with a huge shift from "unemployed" to "incapacitated" recipients:

○ In the mid-1980s there were 3.0m unemployed and 1.1m on incapacity benefit, total 4.1m.
○ In 2005 there were 0.9m unemployed and 2.7m on incapacity, total 3.6m.

In some economically depressed towns in Wales and the North so many locals are apparently incapacitated that the UN should be declaring an international emergency and sending in medical aid. The UK government has now belatedly acknowledged the scam and is introducing tighter policing under a welfare reform billed as "the right to enter the world of work".

The reality around welfare spending is that hard-nosed clarity of purpose and persistent policing get results. And governments around the world have in fact got much harder nosed.

In the US welfare has been reformed radically over the last 15 years, starting under Bill Clinton's presidency and driven largely at state level, building on early innovation in states like Wisconsin. There were initial fears that an entire welfare safety net was being dismantled with terrible consequences for the poor, unemployed and disadvantaged, particularly poor single mothers. In fact the new incentives to find work have had great success, reconnecting welfare recipients with better work and prospects, while also reducing welfare spending.

So this part of public-sector cost management is tricky and politically very sensitive, but it is achievable.

PUBLIC-SECTOR EMPLOYEES

In Chapter 4 I set out four main reasons why managing people cost is so problematic:

○ **Stickiness** – once people are on the payroll it's hard to get them off even if they are poor performers. Nobody likes being the bad guy, firing people.
○ **Relentless cost growth** – wages increase at 1–2% a year faster than inflation; in service activities managing payroll is the biggest cost issue.
○ **Size** – real people cost is a lot larger than it seems when you include all related and long-term costs, like pension liabilities.
○ **Headcount multiplication** – you hire one person, then you find out three months later that the first thing she's done is hire a department around her.

These problems are even bigger in the public sector. The absence of a profit imperative means that nasty people decisions will be ducked and dived around and deferred as long as possible. People will be sidelined and shuffled into make-work jobs rather than fired.

Without the profit measure, managerial status is still often measured by size of department, with increasing headcount seen as a sign of success. Pressure on pay, performance and productivity is weaker than in the private sector.

The hidden cost of a public-sector job is also much worse. Long-term pension and retirement healthcare benefits are never accounted for properly in government accounts. If properly recognized they would contribute up to 20% extra to the real annual cost of a state employee, and they would add staggering sums to the national government debt. In the UK, for example, unrecognized and unfunded state worker pension obligations would represent somewhere between 50% and 100% of GDP. If any private business tried this accounting trick it would be a front-page scandal.

Lastly, most government activity would be classified as services in the private sector, and it has been much harder to get productivity gains in services than in manufacturing.

As well as facing these normal problems of people cost management, the public sector faces additional challenges all of its own.

Most state services are monopolies. With no shareholders, excess monopoly returns can accrue only to the workforce, as above-market wages or better job protection. The government manager, representing the taxpayer, has to battle constantly against this tendency, but these efforts will never be as effective as true competition.

Government attitudes to controlling public-sector pay are conflicted by the "client-voter" problem. When 20–30% of the labor force are working for the state, that's a big share of the public vote, with a strong interest in defending their pay and prospects. Gains for the other 70–80% of taxpayers are more diffuse and longer term, not such a strong motivator in the ballot box.

There can be a confusion between service goals and public policy goals. So a government department of employment whose public policy goal is to help minimize unemployment might be reluctant to cut its own workforce in the interests of service efficiency.

Overall, a job in the public sector may end up being a softer option, and a more lucrative one, than in the private sector – and management change is harder to achieve. Here are some indicative stats from Matthew Elliott and Lee Rotherham in their enjoyable, foaming-at-the-mouth book *The Bumper Book of Government Waste*:

○ The average salary for advertised public-sector jobs in the UK in 2005 was £35,500 ($71,000), which was £10,000 ($20,000) more than the average private-sector wage.
○ Comparing the public vs private sectors, absenteeism is 11 days vs 8, weekly hours worked are 37.6 vs 40.5, retirement is at 60 vs 65, the percentage in final-salary pension schemes is 88% in the public sector vs 16% in the private sector.
○ With a pleasant irony, one of the highest "sickie" rates is at the Department for Work and Pensions, almost 13 days a year,
○ The real total cost of a Member of the European Parliament is £2.4m ($4.8m) a year! (Yes, that's not a typo.)

The authors conclude that "the real root of the problem in public waste comes from the non-jobs, absenteeism and generous pensions that bedeck the entire public sector workforce". You could put equal emphasis on productivity, cost creep, monopoly and the client-voter problem. But the core point is correct: the main challenge in public-sector cost is managing the cost of the public-sector labor force.

PURCHASES FROM EXTERNAL SUPPLIERS

The state is a huge buyer of products and services: hospital catering, garbage collection, prescription drugs, military hardware, IT contracts and enormous infrastructure projects like roads and airports.

Government should be an efficient purchaser. It has the scale to extract maximum buying clout. It represents zero credit risk for a

HOW NOT TO MANAGE PUBLIC-SECTOR COST

The UK in the Labour government's second term under Tony Blair provides the most bizarre case study in how to mess up public-sector cost management.

Labour came to power in 1997 after 18 years in the political wilderness, determined to avoid being seen as dodgy on economic management, its old Achilles' heel. So government spending in its first term was held in an even tighter grip than it had been under the Tories: close to zero real growth, so a steady slight decline as a percentage of GDP. The then Chancellor Gordon Brown was cementing his reputation as "Prudence".

Then, after election to a second term, there was a radical change of tack. Labour announced a four-year wave of "investment" (i.e. massive spending increases) in the public sector, focusing particularly on the National Health Service (NHS) but with big dollops of cash for most departments. From 2001 to 2005 government spending grew at 6% per annum, increasing the state's share of GDP by 5% or +1% a year. Even worse in terms of dead-weight legacy was a reversal of trend in public-sector employment. This had peaked at 7.4m in 1979, the year Thatcher came to power, and then been steadily pared back down to 5m by 1998. By 2007 it had returned to over 6m.

After four years of Happy Days Are Here Again, there was another radical change of tack. As of 2008 we are in a new Ice Age of public spending, with Prime Minister Gordon Brown committed to slashing spending growth to 2% per annum, i.e. zero in real terms, including below-inflation pay increases. The unions are shouting shock and betrayal and mobilizing their strike committees. It will be hard to ratchet pay expectations back down after the years of profligacy.

There are two very bizarre aspects to this whole story. This spending approach flies in the face of common-sense wisdom about how to step up investment, including Gordon Brown's own stated views on the general economy. Even if you were to accept the need to increase public-sector spending, a rapid boom-and-bust cycle is a bad way to do it. In the boom phase there is inadequate institutional capacity to manage the growth and spend the funds effectively. Much of the money gets squandered. A lot, certainly over half, gets grabbed as pay increases for existing staff. Everybody knows that the investment tap can get cut off in the next budget so everybody wants to get their slice now, even if it can't be spent effectively. In the bust phase staff are even more disillusioned and demotivated, because annual expectations have been ramped up. Smaller but steadier step-ups in spending are much easier to manage and get the desired outcomes.

The second oddity is that in almost every other advanced economy, and particularly in continental Europe, the direction of public spending as a percentage of GDP is clearly downward, after painful experiments in the other direction in previous decades – and this change has general public support. The contrast between the UK and Germany is striking. Around 2000 Germany was stuck in low growth, high unemployment and diminishing competitiveness, with a government share of GDP hanging dangerously close to 50%. The UK was flying high on every measure and its government share of GDP was around 40%. Six years later the two economies had moved in opposite directions on government spending. The latest OECD figures show the German percentage as lower than the UK's, 45% vs 46%. We are seeing a resurgence in German economic performance – not yet a transformation, but a reversal of years of disappointment. The UK is not yet in stagnation territory, but the route it has taken is questionable.

supplier. If it needs to finance a purchase it can raise funding at a lower cost of capital than private businesses. So any purchasing failure that we do find in the public sector is an issue of execution, not (as with public-sector employment) an issue of fundamental contradictions and difficulties.

And purchasing failures we do find, unfortunately, by the truckload. Case after case shows that there is tremendous opportunity to improve this aspect of public-sector cost performance:

○ **Military procurement** has been a standing joke since Napoleon. Tales of $1,000 screws abound and defrauding the Pentagon has always been a popular game. Recently a small parts company, C&D Distributors, shipped three machine screws at $1.31 each to marines in Iraq, then charged the US government $455,000 for transport costs – and got paid!

○ Local government has been encouraged to move to **outsourcing** of services like catering. However, its staff often lack the procurement skills to make the best use of competition. Think of the 25-year contracts on catering services for school dinners I mentioned in Chapter 5.

○ **Big flagship construction and infrastructure investments** – oh dear. Just the announcement of a new one can cause mass depression. The new Scottish Parliament building in Edinburgh was budgeted at £40m ($80m) and came in at £400m ($800m). The Big Dig highway project in Boston finished $11bn over budget. Both Montreal Olympic Stadium and Sydney Olympic Park suffered significant cost overruns, and Londoners take a morbid pleasure in the escalating cost farce of the 2012 Olympics.

○ **Public-sector consulting and IT projects** – almost always disastrous and costing far too much money.

STRUCTURAL COST PROBLEMS: HEALTHCARE AND PENSIONS

These two big chunks of state spending are very hard to control, like trying to push water uphill.

State-paid pensions were conceived after the Second World War, when an average working man retired at 65 and died two years later. Women lived longer, but they were only a small percentage of the pensionable workforce.

Since then life expectancy has leapt up, increasing by about two years every decade (and amazingly is still continuing that rate of increase). So two years of happy retirement after 65 have become 10, 15, 20 years or more. Even if pension cost per year had been held constant, total government spend per person would have gone up many times over the last few decades and will continue to go up until state pensions are "reformed" – by raising entitlement age, reducing payment levels or increasing offsetting contributions during the working lifetime.

So far most governments have fudged this issue or nibbled away at the margins, but the sums are such that the next generation of young taxpayers will probably revolt under an increasing transfer burden. (They'd better not revolt until I get mine.)

Healthcare is the other big cost-escalation monster. Healthcare's share of GDP is on a relentless upward spiral – increasing in the US (where the healthcare burden is not a public cost) from 7% in 1970 to over 16% today and set to hit 20% or more by 2020. 20% of GDP, one in five of all dollars earned and spent! Other countries are at lower levels but the trend is the same.

Here the problem is ever-growing demand for increasingly innovative but very expensive medical treatments – drugs, surgery, genetics, long-term care. Increasing life expectancy has some impact on healthcare but it is not the main driver of cost escalation; on average the majority of an individual's lifetime healthcare cost occurs in the last year of life, and that is true whether the last year is at age 65 or age 85.

When the state has accepted the role of main healthcare provider, with the intent of providing universal access to good basic care regardless of ability to pay – which it has in almost all Western European countries and Canada – then it has taken on an unending and irresolvable cost challenge.

OTHER INTRINSIC PROBLEMS WITH PUBLIC-SECTOR COST

The public sector lacks the real market mechanisms that drive efficiency and innovation in the private sector: profit objectives and competition. Is a private business delivering good products or services at a competitive cost and price? If not, it will be obvious quickly on the P&L and customers will switch from any business that becomes sloppy or expensive. Public-sector activities have no such simple measure of success and their customers usually have no competitor they could switch to. So the public sector has to wrestle with indirect ways of stimulating performance improvement, like output and quality targets, or creating internal competition, like league tables of hospitals and schools. These pseudo markets may be better than nothing, but they have philosophical and operational problems and are nowhere near as effective as true markets.

Or take feedback mechanisms. Private-sector customers can vote with their feet very quickly and switch suppliers. Businesses track their profitability daily and report to shareholders every three months. A decline in performance usually triggers a serious response. There is not that much organizational distance between the CEO of a major retailer and a store manager. Feedback loops are rapid, direct, fact based and highly visible.

In the public sector it takes much longer to find out what is happening and to make or demand changes. Customers can only vote every four years; and then they cannot vote specifically as a customer on whether education is being run well, they have to combine in that one vote their view on the Iraq war, on climate change, on abortion

MONSIEUR THATCHER?

Will Nicolas Sarkozy, elected President in 2007, be France's Margaret Thatcher? Half the French population hopes he will, the other half are throwing darts at his photo and planning *manifestations et grèves*. In two days in September 2007, after a quiet start, Sarkozy launched his main attack on France's bloated public sector: US-style "workfare" reforms, elimination of super pension entitlements, a steady rundown in the number of civil servants, performance-based pay. The public-sector unions called his speeches "a declaration of war".

Reforming the French public sector could be, depending on your temperament, the most satisfying or the most sickening job on the planet. The Chairman of BNP-Paribas said: "For the past 25 years, every time a new problem has emerged, our country has responded by increasing government spending." One tiny data point: over the last 20 years, while French agricultural employment has halved, the number of staff in the French Ministry of Agriculture has actually increased!

and so on. Useful performance reporting may be non-existent, late, inconsistent, subject to heavy political spin. Politicians prefer working to very extended delivery timeframes – five- or ten-year programs whose implementation and outcome will be hard to track through the mists of time. Tough underlying performance issues are deferred unless there is a real crisis. And tremendous organizational distance exists between where funding decisions are made and where operations are carried out, between politicians and aides and the manager of a local service.

Tony Blair, who talked a lot about public-sector reform in his ten years as Prime Minister but (in his own judgment) achieved not much of it, gave a parting summary of four core, hard-earned lessons, as reported in *The Economist*:

○ Bottom-up pressure to improve comes from giving consumers of services either choice or (if not possible, e.g. the police) "voice".
○ There must be the spur of competition: purchasers of services must be able to choose among competing providers.
○ Public services must be constantly developing new capabilities and patterns of working, e.g. family physicians carrying out diagnostics and minor surgeries that used to be done in hospitals.
○ Too many centrally imposed targets are dangerous but some elements of top-down performance management are needed, including the setting of minimum standards and performance assessment. Direct interventions can work in rooting out the seriously bad, e.g. failed schools.

Applying the Cost Manager's Toolkit

Most of the themes of the cost manager's toolkit translate directly into the public sector.

LEADERSHIP
○ A challenging base case
○ Individual accountability
○ Persistence
○ A continuous improvement culture
○ Short timeframes
○ Feedback loops
○ Strategic skepticism
○ Top team – finance, HR
○ Role models

This is a good starting checklist for a reform-minded cost manager. The status quo would be a list of the *opposite* of these virtuous attributes. The public sector tends to:

○ Not set up a challenging base case – accepting the current situation and historical cost momentum, not challenging why and how things are done.

○ Not have clear individual accountability – rather a mix of elected ministers, back-office aides and line managers, with frequent reshuffles, reorganizations and multiple reports.

○ Lack persistence and a CI culture – this is really the core problem. Tough cost management tends to occur only in response to emergencies (like New York City in the 1970s or the UK in the early 1980s). Things revert to a non-tough normal as soon as possible.

○ Shy away from short timeframes – cost programs are always announced as something like "a 10% saving over five years", in the hope that quiet attrition will save the day or the targets will vanish in the mists.

○ Avoid strong feedback loops – in particular anything that gives real visibility on progress to the general public.

○ Be a sucker for large strategic projects – big-bang solutions announced with great fanfare but poor execution.

○ Not be great role models – British MPs fought tooth and nail not to disclose details of their personal expenses, information that politicians in the US have had to release for years under freedom of information legislation.

TECHNIQUES AND TACTICS
○ Understanding cost dynamics
○ Management accounts and metrics
○ Bang for buck
○ Slice and dice
○ Understanding natural cost trends
○ Cash cost vs P&L cost
○ Best practice
○ Competitive analysis

As taxpayer-shareholders we need much better metrics around the performance of public services. Penetrating the numbers we do get is like wading through treacle, unlike the accessible reporting and relatively clear accounting and reporting of the private sector (OK, Enron excluded). Most government figures are produced in-house by the departments being measured. There are frequent redefinitions of "inflation", "the economic cycle", "unemployment". We need more thoughtful and useful metrics and we need them prepared and published by an independent statistics and audit body.

In a similar vein, government should adopt private-sector accounting principles. The general public are outraged by public companies' off-balance-sheet financing tricks or pension deficits. They should also be outraged by government off-balance-sheet scamming or by the zero accounting recognition of public-sector pension and healthcare liabilities – no private company would now be allowed to get away with such distortions of reality.

Much more use can be made of competitive analysis. Since government services are usually local monopolies, "competition" here means other countries. For example, the number of Central Bank staff per thousand population is staggeringly wide: 4 in the UK, 8 in the US, 18 in the Eurozone and 57 in Russia. On the face of it you could cut Russia's Central Bank staff by over 90% and the Eurozone's by over 75%. Inside the Eurozone some countries are even more top heavy: the Bank of France still has 14,000 staff compared with the Bank of England's 2,000, even though it has handed monetary policy over to the European Central Bank!

PEOPLE
○ Hiring
○ Paying
○ Technology and productivity
○ Firing
○ Minimizing the core

This is the hardest part of public-sector cost management, twice as hard as it is in the private sector – and it isn't easy there.

The most critical actionable point is the last: minimize the core organization. The state will never be a very effective manager of people cost. The best solution is to push as much of the payroll as possible out into the private sector. Multiple service providers can compete for the state's business, bringing the benefits of competition and profit discipline and removing the moral hazard of client-employee-voters. The state's share of GDP might not change, but its share of employment would change significantly, with big potential efficiencies.

When I was a young whipper-snapper during Thatcher's privatizations in the 1980s I had not understood this logic. So I agreed with privatizing obviously competitive businesses like British Airways and British Telecom, but I could not understand why we would be privatizing monopolies like the water companies or British Rail. I understand now and I agree with it: even a natural monopoly was better in the private sector, on the private-sector payroll. The risk of companies exploiting monopoly could be controlled by regulation. (That British Rail has ended up a financial and operational mess is a regulatory failure, not a counter-argument to privatization.) A far greater risk was the likelihood of a public-sector workforce extracting monopoly returns at the expense of their customers and taxpayers. This can be seen in the intense hostility of public-sector unions to even modest outsourcing moves.

SUPPLIERS
- ○ Playing the balance of power
- ○ Fewer better suppliers
- ○ Intelligent negotiation
- ○ Avoiding lock-in
- ○ Managing total cost of ownership

○ Tough on services cost
○ Reducing non-labor overhead

The public sector needs to become much better at procurement and project management. This is not rocket science. It does not tread on political sensitivities. It does not involve confronting public-sector unions. It is just about getting the right commercial skills in place, being clear on the right principles and establishing good controls.

This is critical as a corollary to minimizing the core organization. It is no good getting the public-sector payroll down if all potential gains are given away in bad outsourcing contracts. And it has to be got right if governments continue to experiment with complex public-and-private structures, like Private Finance Initiatives. (Under a PFI a private firm contracts with the government to build something like a school, hospital or road, and then to maintain it, maybe for decades. The government argument for doing this is that the private sector will be more efficient. The unstated reason is that PFIs take big chunks of infrastructure financing off the public-sector balance sheet.) Bad PFI contracts could be creating huge deadweight burdens for the future: long-term lock-ins at high prices with poor quality controls.

There are very positive role models out there showing what can be done with good procurement and project management, even when dealing with the most complex and political major projects. Probably the most inspiring story is the Delhi Metro. India's track record on public infrastructure is appalling: the Kolkata Metro, for example, had only 17km built in 22 years, with 14 upward budget revisions, massive cost escalation and money disappearing down rabbit holes. Everybody expected the worst in Delhi but it has been a blazing beacon of hope: 65km built so far in less than ten years, three years ahead of schedule, absolutely on budget, everything working, no scandals. The project director Elattuvalapil Sreedharan has almost god-like status in India and was declared "Indian of the

Year" in 2007. Indians would like to clone him and have him run every highway and airport project in the country – or even better, run the country.

WIRED AND GLOBAL
○ The internet – costs of interaction
○ Globalization – the China card
○ Globalization – the India card

The internet is being embraced enthusiastically by central and local governments. All the excitement is around the idea of e-government: online information, self-help, surveys, databases, online filing, online services. And there have already been tremendous successes, transforming the customer experience for users of government services.

Take the example of Washington, DC. The home of the White House and the Lincoln Memorial was also a synonym for corrupt and inefficient government (and coke-sniffing mayors). But recently its new portal, dc.gov, has become a model of e-government, allowing citizens to go online for almost all interactions: getting information, filing forms, obtaining permits, booking appointments, seeing planning applications.

E-government (and i-government, and m-government in India, where more citizens are likely to interact via mobile phones) has already made radical improvements in the customer experience. But in a way that is the easy part. Government has improved service but added the (quite low) cost layer of e-government onto its existing cost base. It has not yet progressed to addressing the radical cost-reduction opportunities on offer.

Just as in online banking and retailing, the internet can drive down the cost of interactions to close to zero. Analysis by Tameside Borough Council in the UK calculated the cost of customer/tax-payer contact as £15 face to face, £1.40 via a telephone call center, and £0.25 for online self-help. This is the kind of analysis that financial services firms did ten years ago. The next step is obvious: government will no longer need the millions of employees now doing face-to-face visits or managing warehouses of paper records. This bullet has yet to be bitten.

The bigger opportunity is to join up e-government with back-office IT. This will be one of the core platforms for a revolution in public services productivity, but it will not be popular with public-sector unions.

Globalization is also going to be a tricky sell. A common reaction is: why should "our" jobs be sent offshore by "our" government? Some US states have experimented with offshoring and quickly backtracked. It's hard to imagine a rapid migration of federal tax authorities to Chennai, even though that is exactly what banks like HSBC and Citi are doing with their back offices.

One India card could, maybe surprisingly, be played earlier: the offshoring of healthcare. There is already strong growth in health-care tourism for expensive hospital operations, to India and to other offshore centers. This could broaden into long-term care, for recovery, chronic illness and possibly old age. When I slide into mental and physical decline I'd prefer to be pleasantly out of it on a sunny beach in Kerala than in a chilly pebbledash care home in Eastbourne. I could be on webcam via Skype with the kids every day for free.

LATERAL THINKING
- Time is money
- Complexity is expensive
- Quality cuts cost
- Let customers do the work
- Turn cost into revenue

Hmm. "Turn cost into revenue"? Parking fines, speed cameras, $500 for an identity card…

"Let customers do the work"? Queuing for six hours in the rain outside the Indian High Commission to get a business visa...

Maybe we don't want the public sector doing that much lateral thinking.

The Public-Sector Opportunity

The rule of thumb that you can almost always cut costs by 15% probably applies in the public sector. 15% in the UK would mean £75bn ($150bn), 6% of GDP. If the public sector got bought by a private equity firm they would find that 15%. As taxpayer-shareholders we should be agitating to get the same amount.

Despite all the difficulties described in this chapter, many industrialized countries have succeeded in dragging state spending down. Germany has embarked on a steady reform program and has been successfully chipping away at the public-sector share of GDP. France may be about to do the same under President Sarkozy.

An ECB economics research paper evaluated the impact of public spending reforms on overall economic growth and on societal health. Its conclusions were:

○ Expenditure reform was generally accompanied by a significant recovery in trend growth and employment, especially in countries that undertook ambitious reforms... was correlated with improvements in indicators of institutional quality... and did not coincide with less favourable developments of human development indicators [including income inequality].
○ Early and persistent [ambitious] reformers have benefited most.
○ There is no evidence that expenditure reductions strongly hurt public education or investment.
○ Available evidence indicates that countries that have lower levels of public expenditure as shares of GDP do a better job at

targeting public transfers toward those at the bottom of the income distribution.

○ Governments can be much leaner and yet equally effective in attaining their basic objectives if they focus on providing a functioning administration that protects property rights and the rule of law, and on supporting the provision of essential public goods (including infrastructure and basic schooling) and basic social safety nets.

The economic turnaround of the Anglo-Saxon reformers has been particularly impressive. New Zealand reversed decades of steep relative economic decline through cutting state spending by around 15% of GDP over two decades. Ireland, which reduced expenditure by the same percentage, has gone from being one of the poorest European economies to having one of the highest incomes per head. Canada, which cut its public-sector share of GDP from 53% to 42%, has recently been outpacing its powerhouse southern neighbor.

When you get better efficiency and productivity in state spending, you get a kick-up in long-term growth across the whole economy. And if you do it well you don't need to make any unpleasant trade-offs around social support and institutional investment; in fact, you get more resources and better social outcomes.

Conclusion: The Cost Manager as Hero

This book has set out a structured, practical approach to intelligent cost management. This is a central subject and challenge for businesses, but one that lacks good general coverage in the literature of management.

I have tried to make the book relevant to managers at every level and in every function. As I argued up front, cost management is not an issue only for the CEO or for senior managers. Junior managers who are tight on cost are learning good habits for the future, ones that will bring them recognition and advance their climb up the organization. Senior managers promote people who make tough decisions themselves and take full responsibility for those decisions. And cost management is not an issue only for functions like finance or production control. The HR department's task today is to help manage that most difficult cost category, people cost.

Cost management really is strategic. It is not a question of choosing between growth and cost cutting. Being a good cost manager gives you the platform to be strategic. It buys you time to make mistakes and build revenue, margin to outprice the competition, funds to outinvest them. And cost management is not just for downturns but for always. Cost strategies and growth strategies are joined at the hip.

I want to reinforce the point that there is intelligent cost management and there is bad cost management. It would be immoral to cut costs in a way that increases risk for customers, for staff or for society

at large. Bad cost cutting would be unethical and actually uneconomic – the potential cost of any disaster would overwhelm the
short-term savings. And it would be near-sighted and stupid not to
put a high value on relationships and trust: caring for customers and
nurturing employees are not at odds with good cost management.

An intelligent cost cutter needs to be able to distinguish good
investment in future growth from bad excessive cost today. You can
always hack costs like marketing, new business development, early-
stage investments. But although good cost management is a necessary characteristic of a great company, it is not sufficient. Great
companies need profitability now *and* platforms for future growth.

I'll conclude with a quick roundup of the topics:

O **Cost Leadership**: I looked at how the top team – the CEO,
  COO, business unit heads, the heads of finance and HR – needs
  to take the lead and set the tone on cost.
O **Techniques and Tactics**: I laid out a set of ideas, approaches,
  tips and tricks that I have found effective in cost-reduction programs and in ongoing cost management.
O **People**: I tackled the most difficult and most critical cost area,
  full-time staff.
O **Suppliers**: I covered all other cost categories, from raw materials
  to outsourced services.
O **Cost Cutting Case Study**: I gave a blow-by-blow account of a
  four-month cost-reduction project I managed at the European
  operations of a business services company that had been bought
  by a private equity firm.
O **Wired and Global**: I explored two of today's high-profile cost-
  reduction themes that have huge potential: the internet and
  globalization.
O **Lateral Thinking**: I turned some conventional thinking about
  cost on its head, looking at the sneaky ways cost can get created
  and creative ways it can be cut.

○ **Cost Management as Strategy**: I discussed how good cost management can underpin business strategy, including acquisitions, pricing and growth.

○ **Cost in the Public Sector**: I used the analytical framework of the previous chapters to look at government spending.

Good cost management is not just the dry, Dark Side of business. Good cost management can be heroic.

There is an American cartoon strip that involves a publishing firm of birds. The boss owl calls his staff together to tell them he's decided to bring in a productivity consultant. "You can come in now, Conan," he calls out in the last panel, and there's the barbarian himself, axe over shoulder.

The cartoonist is thinking of Conan as the bad guy, the destroyer. Actually, Conan is the *hero*. In his Marvel comics incarnation of the 1960s he may be a wine-swilling, wench-grabbing, bone-crushing brute, but he is also at heart a *good guy*, opposed to the dark forces of sorcery, cannibalism and reptilian cults.

Conan was particularly strong on specific bits of the cost manager's toolkit:

○ **Persistence** – he just kept on bashing away, no matter what the odds.

○ **Minimizing the core organization** – Conan traveled alone; even Red Sonja couldn't get a full-time job with him.

○ On the spectrum of **cutting vs managing** he was probably better at short-term cost-reduction programs than managing prudently for the long haul.

○ **Slicing and dicing** were his specialty!

He understood very well the enormous strategic value of being cheaper *and* better. He was the Dell of the mercenary-barbarian market segment. All he needed for expenses was a camp fire, a flagon of mead and a servant girl. But he could hack his way past enemy hordes and giant serpents better than anyone.

Could we ask for a better summary of good cost management?

The Cost Manager's Toolkit

Laptop-size Summary

LEADERSHIP

A challenging base case	Make the base case (for annual budgets and cost reviews) always a challenging one
	Constantly push the organization to be more cost efficient – this year not next year
	Make sure your direct reports expect that attitude, so they no longer come in with anything less aggressive
Individual accountability	Be absolutely clear which individual manager is 100% responsible for hitting each cost target
	Eliminate joint or fuzzy accountabilities
Persistence	Make sure the organization knows that you will always persist in the drive for cost efficiencies
	Don't forget commitments or let targets drift – don't be deflected with half measures
Continuous improvement	Establish a continuous improvement culture
Short timeframes	Set short-term targets for concrete progress
	Follow up at short intervals – what progress has been made today? This week?

LEADERSHIP (cont.)

Feedback loops	Make sure there is a process for seeing quickly and clearly what progress is being made on cost targets...
	...Involving good hard data, delivered quickly, reviewed frequently, with visibility and transparency
Strategic skepticism	Make your managers very nervous about proposals to invest in strategic partnerships or core competencies
Top team	Establish a strong CFO and finance function, the CEO's critical right hand for cost management
	And a proactive, hard-nosed HR function, willing to take on the key issues of people cost and staff productivity
Role models	You and your top managers should be good role models in personal expense habits
	Establish fairness or equality in expense policies and behavior down through the organization
	Create a head office environment that sends the right cost message to suppliers and employees

TECHNIQUES AND TACTICS

Understanding cost dynamics	Understand what creates cost
	And what your key trends are (up and down)
	And how costs move in relation to decisions and activities, e.g. with revenue and headcount
Management accounts and metrics	Produce management accounts and metrics that let you understand, model and manage the true economics
	Make the presentation crisp and accessible
Bang for buck	Focus on where to get the biggest results fastest
Slice and dice	Break out and chisel away at the difficult costs
	Unbundle activities and map them against customer segments
Understanding natural cost trends	Don't fool yourself you are pushing water downhill
	Don't expect to push water uphill
Cash cost not P&L cost	Particularly in a cash crunch
Best practice	Regularly look for best practice across the organization
	Take opportunities to do experiments and comparisons
Competitive analysis	Check competitors' cost positions and trend – have they found more cost-effective ways of working?
	Distinguish structural cost differences from operational execution

PEOPLE

The basics	Recognize that people costs are sticky, go up relentlessly and are always larger than you think
	Get a strong cost-oriented HR function to play a lead role in managing people cost
Hiring	Capitalize hiring decisions like capital investments
	Minimize risk, maximize flexibility
Paying	Hold your nerve, stay firm
	Watch out for the salary survey cost escalator
	Don't look to variable compensation programs for cost reduction
Technology and productivity	Constantly look for ways to transform productivity
	First without new technology – don't automate bad practice
	Secondly with new technology – including ways of eliminating an activity completely
	Require line managers to do zero-based reviews of activities
	Get CIOs and IT heads to trawl for new ideas
Firing	Clear out dead wood, the organization will thank you
	Do it proactively, earlier rather than later
	Prune with a rolling two-year forced ranking
	Stick to a rigorous appraisal and review process
	Watch out for taskforce volunteers

PEOPLE (cont.)

Minimize the core organization	Push component supply and low-value functions out to subcontractors and outsourcers
	Replace empire building with a minimize-core mindset
	Build flat organizations not pyramids

SUPPLIERS

Understand and play the balance of power	High interdependence
	High buyer dependence
Supplier consolidation	Move to fewer better suppliers
Intelligent negotiation	Understand supplier economics
	Try to find win–wins
	Leave profit for the supplier
	Consolidate buying power
	Trade off prices and terms
Don't get locked in	Have one credible alternative
	Reduce switching cost
	Avoid long-term contracts
	Maintain an active marketplace
Manage TCO	Total cost of ownership
Get tough on services cost	Central procurement
	Professional services
	Outsourcing
	Travel
	Marketing
	IT

SUPPLIERS (cont.)

Reduce non-labor overhead	Vendor price
	Quantities and frequencies
	Insource or outsource
	Property utilization
	Management accountability and reporting

WIRED AND GLOBAL

The internet	Pursue the cost-reduction opportunities offered by the internet, creatively and relentlessly
	Get all line managers thinking about how the internet could change the costs of interacting with suppliers, employers, current and potential customers
Globalization	Pursue the cost-reduction opportunities offered by globalization of production – the China card
	And for the globalization of services – the India card: IT, back office, customer service, sales and marketing, R&D

LATERAL THINKING

Time is money	Speed up all business processes
	Reduce cycle time to save cost
Complexity is expensive	Cut costs by simplifying what you do and how you do it
	If complexity is deliberate, make sure value exceeds cost
	Can you get most of the value but with lesser cost?
Quality cuts cost	Invest more up front in quality to get an overall reduction in cost
	Reduce back-end costs like quality control, rework, service recovery, product recalls
Let customers do the work	Identify activities and costs that customers could do better and more cheaply
	And/or things that customers would actually prefer to do for themselves
Turn cost into revenue and profit	Turn cost lines into revenue
	Use menu pricing to lower net costs, for you and for customers
	Get for free things you now pay for or, even better, get people to pay you
	Turn cost centers into profitable third-party businesses

COST MANAGEMENT AS STRATEGY

Deliver value via acquisitions	Most acquisitions don't add value, but a strong cost manager has a much better chance of doing so
	Cost-based synergies are better than revenue- or scope-based synergies
Underpin pricing strategies	In price wars – for market leaders and market attackers
	In new product introductions – pricing down the experience curve
	In long-term customer contracts – making profitable commitments
Discover more new growth opportunities	Drive down the cost of discovery
	Retain more equity value
Create an effective center in a large corporation	Make decentralization the default position
	Establish a clear supplier–customer relationship between the center and the business units
	Be particularly hard on center cost creep
	Establish and track hard metrics around center efficiency
	Do annual private equity-type reviews that challenge the center

Index

1 Acknowledgments

My thanks to:

Nick, Sally and Victoria at Nicholas Brealey Publishing, who have been fantastic in their support and value-added.

Richard Koch, for early enthusiasm and introductions.

Chris Outram and Mark Jannaway of OC&C Strategy Consultants, for ideas and debate, particularly regarding supplier management.

Many consulting clients whose projects have given me much of the rich experience and case study material in the book, in particular recently (without associating them in any way with the ideas and any errors in the book, with which they may disagree and which are my responsibility alone): David Jones of Amadeus, Geoff Cooper of Travis Perkins, and Pradeep Singh of Aditi Technologies.